PRINCESS MARGARET

'Honest and chivalrous . . . a book which deserved
to be written'

Books and Bookmen

'Fairly written . . . dignity is restored'
The Economist

'The author has accomplished a delicate task with
sympathy and tact'

This England

'A deeply absorbing study'

Majesty Magazine

'Warwick seems to have enjoyed the Princess's
confidence and he has written his apologia well'
Times Literary Supplement

'An excellent book . . . like a breath of good, clean
fresh air'

Oxford Times

'This book differs from previous enterprises in that
it is the first in which the Princess has helped the
author'

The Times

'The most authentic account so far of her public
and private life'

The Star

'Mr Warwick has produced a long overdue defence of a much-maligned Princess'

The Listener

'What spills out of Christopher Warwick's biography is the bitter waste of Margaret the woman'

Daily Express

'A timely and sympathetic biography'

Financial Times

'Detailed research adds a fascinating overview to new insights'

Fair Lady Magazine

ABOUT THE AUTHOR

Christopher Warwick was born in London in 1949. He has studied royal history since his schooldays and has published two books and numerous articles on the subject. He worked in publishing before becoming a full-time writer, and is the Consultant Editor of *Majesty* magazine. Apart from history and writing, his interests include interior decoration, the arts and English country houses.

Princess Margaret

Christopher Warwick

CORONET BOOKS
Hodder and Stoughton

Copyright © 1983 by Christopher Warwick

First published in Great Britain
1983 by Weidenfeld & Nicolson Ltd

Coronet edition 1984

British Library C.I.P.

Warwick, Christopher
  Princess Margaret.
  1. Margaret, Princess, *Countess of Snowdon*
  I. Title
  941.085'092'4   DA585.A5M3

  ISBN 0-340-35487-9

Printed and bound in Great Britain for
Hodder and Stoughton Paperbacks, a
division of Hodder and Stoughton Ltd,
Mill Road, Dunton Green, Sevenoaks,
Kent (Editorial Office: 47 Bedford
Square, London, WC1 3DP) by
Richard Clay (The Chaucer Press) Ltd,
Bungay, Suffolk

Contents

Author's Note and Dedication

I first met Her Royal Highness The Princess Margaret at the beginning of June 1980 and, as a result of conversations with her, the form of this biography was conceived.

While I cannot claim official status for it and the opinions expressed – unless otherwise indicated – are my own, I have been able to write this book with the advantage of numerous meetings with Her Royal Highness, given with a patience which proved limitless. Throughout this time, Princess Margaret and I were in agreement on most points, but especially where our mutual desire for accuracy was concerned.

I therefore dedicate this book to Her Royal Highness for the trust she has placed in me and by way of thanks for the great compliment she has paid me.

CHRISTOPHER WARWICK

Acknowledgements

While my first thanks are, of course, due to HRH The Princess Margaret, I should like to express my warm gratitude to a number of people who have each made positive contributions to this book. Of the many who gave freely of their time, some asked to remain anonymous and I must respect that wish. Those I am able to thank by name, however, are Roddy and Tania Llewellyn, Jocelyn Stevens, Lord Glenconner and Angela Howard-Johnson. I had hoped that the Earl of Snowdon might accept my invitation to contribute, but for personal reasons he declined to do so.

I am particularly indebted to Brian Auld and Netty Forshaw for their criticism and encouragement, while my parents' enthusiasm has, as always, proved boundless.

The assistance I received from Audrey Russell, Charlotte Balazs, Bettina K. Fredrick, Fella Hughes, Doreen Montgomery, Shirley Russell and Norman McMullen, as well as from my fellow writers and friends Theo Aronson and Dulcie M. Ashdown, proved invaluable and to them all I extend my warmest appreciation.

Of my friends and former colleagues at Weidenfeld & Nicolson, I am no less indebted to Louise Allan-Jones, Bud MacLennan and Hetty Wallace who did so much to help make the hardback edition of this book such a success. Where this edition is concerned, I would like to offer my thanks to Alan Gordon-Walker for his courtesy and co-operation.

C.W.

Family Tree of HRH The Princess Margaret

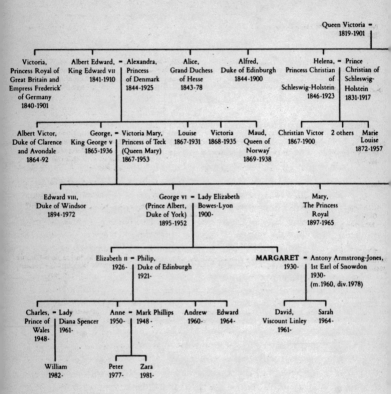

Queen Victoria =
1819-1901

Victoria, Princess Royal of Great Britain and Empress Frederick of Germany 1840-1901

Albert Edward, King Edward VII 1841-1910 = Alexandra, Princess of Denmark 1844-1925

Alice, Grand Duchess of Hesse 1843-78

Alfred, Duke of Edinburgh 1844-1900

Helena, Princess Christian of Schleswig-Holstein 1846-1923 = Prince Christian of Schleswig-Holstein 1831-1917

Albert Victor, Duke of Clarence and Avondale 1864-92

George, King George V 1865-1936 = Victoria Mary, Princess of Teck (Queen Mary) 1867-1953

Louise 1867-1931

Victoria 1868-1935

Maud, Queen of Norway 1869-1938

Christian Victor 1867-1900

2 others

Marie Louise 1872-1957

Edward VIII, Duke of Windsor 1894-1972

George VI (Prince Albert, Duke of York) 1895-1952 = Lady Elizabeth Bowes-Lyon 1900-

Mary, The Princess Royal 1897-1965

Elizabeth II, 1926- = Philip, Duke of Edinburgh 1921-

MARGARET 1930- = Antony Armstrong-Jones, 1st Earl of Snowdon 1930- (m.1960, div.1978)

Charles, Prince of Wales 1948- = Lady Diana Spencer 1961-

Anne 1950- = Mark Phillips 1948-

Andrew 1960-

Edward 1964-

David, Viscount Linley 1961-

Sarah 1964-

William 1982-

Peter 1977-

Zara 1981-

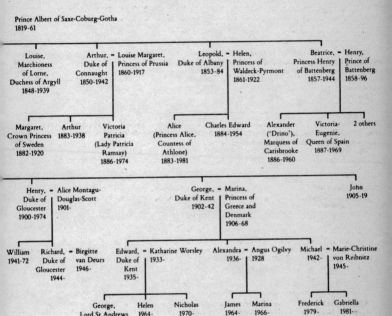

Prince Albert of Saxe-Coburg-Gotha
1819-61

Louise,
Marchioness
of Lorne,
Duchess of Argyll
1848-1939

Arthur, = Louise Margaret,
Duke of   Princess of Prussia
Connaught 1860-1917
1850-1942

Leopold, = Helen,
Duke of Albany Princess of
1853-84   Waldeck-Pyrmont
           1861-1922

Beatrice, = Henry,
Princess Henry Prince of
of Battenberg Battenberg
1857-1944 1858-96

Margaret,
Crown Princess
of Sweden
1882-1920

Arthur
1883-1938

Victoria
Patricia
(Lady Patricia
Ramsay)
1886-1974

Alice
(Princess Alice,
Countess of
Athlone)
1883-1981

Charles Edward
1884-1954

Alexander
('Drino'),
Marquess of
Carisbrooke
1886-1960

Victoria-
Eugenie,
Queen of Spain
1887-1969

2 others

Henry, = Alice Montagu-
Duke of   Douglas-Scott
Gloucester 1901-
1900-1974

George, = Marina,
Duke of   Princess of
Kent   Greece and
1902-42   Denmark
          1906-68

John
1905-19

William
1941-72

Richard, = Birgitte
Duke of   van Deurs
Gloucester 1946-
1944-

Edward, = Katharine Worsley
Duke of   1933-
Kent
1935-

Alexandra = Angus Ogilvy
1936-   1928

Michael = Marie-Christine
1942-   von Reibnitz
         1945-

George,
Lord St Andrews
1962-

Helen
1964-

Nicholas
1970-

James
1964-

Marina
1966-

Frederick
1979-

Gabriella
1981-

PROLOGUE

Not long after I approached Princess Margaret with my proposal for this book, I received an invitation to lunch in order that we could discuss the idea in more detail. I arrived at Kensington Palace on a bright February day in 1981 and walked towards the cobble-stone square that is known as Clock Court. A minute or two later, I was at the top of the short flight of stone steps that leads to the double front doors of the house that is known as apartment 1A.

The butler preceded me across the hall, in which hangs Annigoni's famous portrait of the Princess, to the door of the drawing-room. 'Mr Warwick, Your Royal Highness,' he announced. As I entered, Princess Margaret greeted me with outstretched hand and a broad smile. Although by this time the Princess and I had already met on a number of occasions, I have never ceased to be impressed by her. Indeed I make no apology for saying that Princess Margaret is one of the most fascinating women I have ever known.

'What do you think about Christopher writing this book?' she asked a mutual friend who had joined us. The reply, to my relief, was favourable: 'I think it's a very good idea, Ma'am.' At that moment the doors of the dining-room were opened and luncheon was announced. We took our places at the oval table. I sat, as I was to do on future occasions, at the Princess's left hand, facing the fireplace with its intricate carved relief of oak-leaves and acorns, above which, against a sand-coloured wall, is hung a large oil painting by John Piper.

'Until now I have never co-operated with an author on a book about myself, because I never wanted one to be written,' the Princess said. 'I don't think I'm interesting enough. But look what happens when they try to write about me without my help. Did you listen

1

to me on *Desert Island Discs*?' she asked. 'I said then that I have been misreported and misrepresented since the age of seventeen.'

Inaccurate stories were being told about Princess Margaret even before then, however. Having eaten sparingly, the Princess lit a cigarette in a gold holder and recalled one press story that had angered her when she was fifteen: 'I was with some of my fellow Sea Rangers in a boat on the lake at Frogmore. And *what* do you think appeared in the newspapers? They said I had pulled the bung from the bottom of the boat! That made me frightfully cross. I was part of a *team* and very proud of it, I might tell you. I would never have dreamt of doing something so irresponsible.'

This story was one of the earliest but, like many others that were to follow, it helped build what might best be called 'the Princess Margaret legend'.

An hour or so later we returned to the drawing-room and my fellow guest departed. As she invited me to sit beside her on one of the sofas flanking the open fireplace Princess Margaret asked, 'Do you have time for a talk now?'

Thus began the first of many frank conversations with the Princess which have made this biography possible.

CHAPTER ONE

MARGARET OF YORK

The birth of Princess Margaret in Scotland in the late summer of 1930 was an event of particular distinction, for hers was the first royal birth of any significance to have occurred north of the border for more than three centuries – since the birth of the future King Charles I in 1600.

It is true that Princess Henry of Battenberg, the ninth and last child of Queen Victoria, had given birth to her only daughter Princess Victoria-Eugenie at Balmoral in 1887, but this could barely compare in importance. Princess Victoria-Eugenie was born the thirty-second grandchild of the sovereign and thirty-ninth in line to the throne; Princess Margaret was the second child of the heir presumptive, Prince Albert, Duke of York, and was born fourth in the line of succession. Interestingly, in later years Princess Victoria-Eugenie (who in 1906 married King Alfonso XIII of Spain) and her young relative, Princess Margaret, developed a strong personal bond, celebrating their common country of birth.

Princess Margaret's story begins at Glamis Castle in Tayside. Since 1372 it has been the ancestral home of the Lyon family, later Earls of Strathmore and Kinghorne, and the castle's associations with royalty stretch far into the past. King Malcolm II of Scotland is said to have died there and Shakespeare supposedly set the scene of King Dundan's murder by Macbeth in the castle's old guardroom, now known as Duncan's Hall. Mary, Queen of Scots was once a visitor and so too was the Old Pretender – James VIII of Scotland to his supporters. Today, however, Glamis is associated more with its most famous daughter, Queen Elizabeth the Queen Mother, born Lady Elizabeth

Bowes-Lyon, the ninth child of the fourteenth Earl and Countess of Strathmore and Kinghorne.

Though by birth the Queen Mother is an Englishwoman, by proud inheritance she has always considered herself a Scot. Glamis was the scene of many happy childhood memories for her and when she married the Duke of York, King George V and Queen Mary's second son, in 1923, the couple spent part of their honeymoon at her Scottish family home. It was only natural that seven years later she should wish to pay tribute both to Scotland and to her Bowes-Lyon ancestry by giving birth to her second child at Glamis.

The Duchess of York's decision delighted the Scots, but one Englishman declared that some might consider that the *accouchement* was being conducted in 'an irregular hole-and-corner way'. He was Harry Boyd, the Ceremonial Secretary at the Home Office in London who, with the Home Secretary, J.R. Clynes, would have to travel north for the event. By tradition a Minister of the Crown had to be present at a royal birth as an independent and incorruptible witness. This custom had become firmly established after the so-called 'Warming-pan Incident' of 1688 when Mary of Modena, the second wife of King James II, was accused of having offered a 'changeling' as heir to the throne. The outmoded tradition was eventually abolished by King George VI in 1948, when the then Princess Elizabeth gave birth to Prince Charles, on the grounds that it was neither required nor substantiated by law.

Unlike the royal baby, the Home Secretary and Mr Boyd arrived in Scotland prematurely on 5 August, and had to spend the next sixteen days kicking their heels.

'I feel so sorry for Mr Clynes, having to wait for so long,' wrote the Duke of York to Queen Mary. 'I always wanted him to come up when he was sent for, which would have been so much simpler.'

On the night of Thursday 21 August their patience was rewarded and the following morning the *London Gazette* formally announced: 'Yesterday evening at 22 minutes after 9 o'clock, Her Royal Highness The Duchess of York was safely delivered of a Princess at Glamis Castle. His Royal Highness The Duke of York and the Countess of Strathmore and Kinghorne were present. Mr Secretary Clynes was also present. Her Royal Highness and the Infant Princess are doing perfectly well. . . .'

'Got the news that Elizabeth had a little girl . . .' ran part of King George V's diary entry for 22 August. Later that same day the King with Queen Mary and their fourth son, Prince George, left Sandringham for Glamis and their first peep at the infant.

'E. looking very well and the baby a darling,' declared the Queen in her diary.

In London Princess Margaret's birth was marked by the traditional salutes of gunfire from both Hyde Park and the Tower of London. *The Times* reported that men in the crowd stood bareheaded and 'at the end of the salute there was hearty cheering for the little princess and her mother'. The bells of St Paul's Cathedral and Westminster Abbey were rung in celebration and 'Mayfair was gay with flags on the clubs and shops'.

Messages of congratulation came pouring in. The Prime Minister, Ramsay MacDonald, in office for the second time, sent the Yorks his 'heartiest felicitations'; the armed services despatched congratulations to both parents and royal grandparents; the Dominions took the occasion as an opportunity to send cables couched in tones of happiness and reverence, and civic dignitaries and stuffy corporations followed suit.

It has been said that the Duke and Duchess of York had hoped for a male child this time – a possible future king, for the Prince of Wales, now in his mid-thirties, was still unmarried and it looked increasingly likely that the crown would eventually pass from him to the Duke of York's line. However, though by law the crown passes to the sons of a sovereign before the daughters, even when the latter are older, Britain has never adopted the Salic law by which a woman cannot inherit a throne in her own right, and it is doubtful that the Yorks felt that they had disappointed the nation by producing a second daughter. The Princess's birth meant that the line of succession was now doubly secured and, as such, the occasion was regarded as one of joy. Nowhere was that sentiment echoed more loudly than in the village of Glamis itself.

Heavy rain on the night of the birth meant that the villagers' plans for an immediate celebration had to be postponed, but the following evening, as the crowd was piped to the top of nearby Hunter's Hill, the sky was clear and the success of the gathering was assured. The focal point of the festivities was the lighting of a brushwood beacon by three young girls using the same torches which, seven years earlier, had lit a bonfire celebrating the Duke of York's marriage to Lady Elizabeth Bowes-Lyon.

Attracted by the blaze, which was seen across six counties, excited visitors from as far away as Edinburgh and Aberdeen joined the Glamis villagers as they danced around the fire and refreshed themselves from barrels of beer specially provided by Lord Strathmore, the proud grandfather.

From the grounds of Glamis Castle itself the Duke of York with his parents-in-law watched the reddened sky and it was reported that his elder daughter, the four-and-a-half-year-old Princess Elizabeth, was taken to a window set high in one of the castle's towers to watch the beacon's glow.

Nowadays widespread celebration at the birth of a second daughter to a King's second son would be viewed with some cynicism - at least in certain quarters. But if the joy at Princess Margaret's birth might seem misplaced in the latter half of the century, one has to consider why the event proved such a welcome diversion.

Europe both economically and politically had failed to find stability in the years that followed the Great War. The 1920s and indeed the 1930s are often represented today in a very one-sided manner, highlighting the affluent existence of a small minority and ignoring the lives of the majority. The more realistic face of postwar peace was considerable hardship and confusion, which served to help confound rather than support hopes for a brilliant, unblemished future. The 1914-18 War had been called 'the war to end all wars' and in its wake Britain was to become a land 'fit for heroes to live in', noble sentiments that were quickly followed by disillusionment. The mood was caught in a letter which an ex-soldier wrote to *The Times*. Dated Armistice Day 1919, it read: 'I have today given two minutes praying for our dead, and two hours regretting I am not one of them.'

Peace was born with unemployment as its ugly sister. In 1921 two million people were out of work. Eight years later that figure had dropped to 1.2 million, only to top the two million mark again in 1930, with men spending long hours in even longer dole queues. In the period 1921 to 1929 two ephemeral pacts were made. In 1925 the Locarno Agreement, spelling out a plan for safeguarding world security, was signed and a relieved Winston Churchill wrote of it that 'hope rests on a surer foundation'. During the following year,

Germany, its economy in ruins and its oligarchic Weimar Republic virtually on its knees, was granted membership of the League of Nations. This seemed a sure sign that the enemy had not simply been beaten, but had been won over to help preserve peace and order. Then, in 1928, came the Kellog-Briand Pact, signed by sixty-five nations. For a time this also helped to uphold dreams of everlasting peace. In the end, however, the 'surer foundation' of which Churchill had written amounted to little more than fine rhetoric. Neither pact could fill the stomachs of Britain's hungry or find its people work, prevent the growth of Hitler's National Socialist Party or halt the thuggery of Mussolini's Fascists.

It is not difficult to see why the British people, alarmed by what was happening at home and abroad, and offered bold political speeches rather than tangible solutions by their leaders, would turn towards the Royal Family for reassurance. They at least were a dependable, unifying influence amidst all the disorder and offered hope in a future that otherwise seemed bleak, satisfying people's psychological as well as emotional needs. Indeed, if the Crown was untouchable – as many believed – then it provided a sanctuary that nothing could desecrate.

King George V and Queen Mary appeared as stalwart figures of the old school, unchanging in their behaviour and unbending in their beliefs. If they were remote, that was how the nation wanted them to be, steadfastly upholding values which most people wished to see preserved. The Prince of Wales, on the other hand, symbolized the new trends. So far as royalty went, he was a man ahead of his time, and while his relaxed modern attitude might be anathema to his father, it was an inspiration to his own generation. In time the nation expected him to make an exemplary king and even if he had not yet got round to taking a wife who would make an equally exemplary queen, there was the happy and stable family life of the Duke and Duchess of York to look to for comfort and hope.

Ironically domestic peace and unity within the Royal Family itself were only to exist for a few more years, until it became apparent that the Prince of Wales was intending to marry the divorced American Mrs Simpson. As yet, however, the Prince's taste for married women, which was not common public knowledge, caused no deep concern and there was little to taint the pleasure of the Duke and Duchess of York as their infant daughter made her first journey from Glamis to the family's residence at 145 Piccadilly. This tall, balconied house of grey stone stood on the right of Apsley House, the first Duke of Wellington's mansion at Hyde Park Corner; behind it lay Hamilton Gardens and a little further still, Hyde Park. Sadly, 145 Picadilly was demolished by an enemy bomb in the Second World War and today its foundations lie beneath the course of modern Park Lane.

Even though several weeks had now passed since the Princess's birth, the baby still had no name. 'I am anxious to call her Ann Margaret,' the Duchess wrote to her mother-in-law, Queen Mary, 'as I think Ann of York sounds pretty, and Elizabeth and Ann go so well together. I wonder what you think? Lots of people have suggested Margaret, but it has no family links really on either side.'

It is true that there were no immediate links, but Margaret is an evergreen name in Scotland, honouring the queen who had come to be revered as a saint. It was also a name well rooted in royal history. There was, for example, Margaret of Anjou who in 1444, at the age of fourteen, had married Henry VI; and the wise and scholarly Margaret Beaufort, mother of Henry VII and grandmother of the 'Great Harry', Henry VIII. It was she who had founded colleges at both Oxford and Cambridge, had launched Caxton and his printing presses, and had done much to raise the intellectual – if not the moral – tone of the Tudor court. Nor was it to be overlooked that the young Duchess of York herself was named Marguerite.

In the end it was King George V's insistence that his granddaughter should be called Margaret – and his dislike of the name Ann – that swayed the couple's decision.

'Bertie and I have decided now to call our little daughter Margaret Rose instead of Margaret Ann, as Papa does not like Ann – I hope that you like it. I think it is very pretty together.' This time the tone of the Duchess's letter to her mother-in-law was gentle but above all firm. She and the Duke had now made up their minds and would clearly brook no further objections from the King.

Unlike her father, who was known as Bertie within the family circle, and her sister Elizabeth, who soon became Lilibet, the Princess would nearly always be called by her full name of Margaret, though later Prince Charles's childhood abbreviation to Margot was in turn adopted by Princess Anne and afterwards by Prince Andrew, Prince Edward and the Princess of Wales. However, during her early years the Americans, with their apparent fondness for double forenames, added an imaginary hyphen to the Princess's names and began referring to her as Margaret Rose. The European press followed suit, much to the chagrin of the Princess herself. At about the age of ten, she once complained bitterly to her mother, 'You gave Lilibet three names. Why didn't you give *me* three instead of only two? Margaret Rose!'

The Princess's christening took place at Buckingham Palace in October 1930. Following family tradition, she was carried to the gold, lily-shaped font containing water from the River Jordan dressed in the satin and lace robe first worn by Queen Victoria's eldest child, Vicky (later the Empress Frederick of Germany). Her five sponsors, or god-parents, were Edward, Prince of Wales (known to the family as David), for whom his brother Prince George, later Duke of Kent, stood proxy; the future Queen Ingrid of Denmark, for whom her aunt, Lady Patricia Ramsay, stood proxy; Princess Victoria, the second of George v's three sisters; Lady Rose Leveson-Gower, later the Countess Granville, a sister of the Duchess of York (in honour of whom the infant Princess received her second name); and the Honourable (later Sir) David Bowes-Lyon, the Duchess's youngest brother.

Then, as now, the general public found following royal lives a fascinating occupation and it seemed as if the press and radio could not get enough news of the family life of the Duke and Duchess of York. At home, in Europe and in the United States, the interest in the young Princesses was quite remarkable. Princess Margaret, as the baby, had yet to become a familiar figure and at this time attention was keenly focused on the young Princess Elizabeth or 'Princess Betty' as some American journals were frivolous enough to call her. People sent gifts to her, wrote her letters, avidly collected her pictures and copied her clothes. When she appeared in yellow, for example, the predominant pinks and blues of children's wardrobes all but disappeared. 'It almost frightens me that people should love her so much,' the Duchess of York wrote to Queen Mary.

During the winter of 1931, when Princess Margaret was a little over a year old, the Duke and Duchess of York acquired a country retreat from their London home. Royal Lodge in Windsor Great Park was a comfortable, secluded house commanding a fine view. Originally the *cottage ornée* of the Prince Regent, it had known a succession of tenants before the Yorks took possession. They did not move in, however, until the Duke had sold his six hunting horses in the interests of economy. Nearly £1000 was realized for them at auction, which was a much needed saving.

'It has come as a great shock to me that my hunting should have been one of the things I must do without,' wrote the Duke to the Master of the Pytchley Hunt. In more despondent tone he wrote to a friend about having to face the 'damned hard facts'. The root cause of these 'damned hard facts' had been the collapse of a bank in Vienna, which had repercussions all over Europe, causing further economic depression. In Britain that August, as George V advised his Prime Minister to form an emergency coalition, royal finances did not escape the inevitable process of retrenchment. The King himself surrendered £50,000 of his Civil List allowance, while the Prince of Wales made a corresponding gesture, remitting half of his own revenues to the Treasury.

To quote Queen Mary, 1931 was 'a tiresome year, full of anxieties'. Yet one anxiety that did not prey on her mind – nor on that of the King – was how their granddaughters were to be educated. It has been said, erroneously, that the Duke and Duchess of York considered sending the Princesses to school along with other children. But even if such an idea had entered their heads, the King would never have allowed it. Princes and princesses had always been educated at home and there would be no change now.

That spring Miss Marion Crawford, or Crawfie as she became known, was employed as governess to the Princesses on the recommendation of the Duchess's sister, Lady Rose Leveson-Gower. Crawfie, who had been born in Kilmarnock, but raised in Dunfermline after her widowed mother remarried, was twenty-two. By her own testimony, she had wanted to become a teacher, not a governess, but after sitting her exams at the Moray House Training College in Edinburgh, chance found her invited to teach history on a temporary basis to Lord Bruce, the seven-year-old son of the Earl and Countess of Elgin. Not long afterwards she found herself with another pupil, Mary Leveson-Gower, the young niece of the Duchess of York.

'It seemed to me then,' Crawfie wrote later, 'that this was just a pleasant interlude, a temporary arrangement to fill in the time between one course of study and the next.' In fact, it was to prove very much more than an interlude and, after an introduction to the Duke and Duchess of York, Miss Crawford was invited to become governess to the two Princesses. It was to be a long, harmonious relationship until the Royal Family felt that Miss Crawford had badly let them down by publishing a book about her life with the Princesses, and the expression 'doing a Crawfie' entered the Royal Family's private vocabulary. In the spring of 1931, however, she was warmly welcomed as a member of the York household, despite the misgivings of those – including the King and Queen – who thought her too young for such an important post.

CHAPTER TWO

A HOUSE IN PICCADILLY

The schoolroom at 145 Piccadilly was a small, comfortably furnished room off the Duchess of York's drawing-room. Until Princess Margaret was old enough, it would have but one pupil. Meanwhile, the younger Princess would remain in the nursery watched over by the devoted Clara Knight, once nanny to the Duchess herself, and known as Allah (pronounced 'Ah-là').

As soon as Princess Margaret did start lessons at the age of five, there grew an undisguised rivalry between Allah and Crawfie. Much to the amusement of both Princesses, there raged nothing short of a jealous possessiveness: while the children's nanny could not wait to snatch her charges away from the schoolroom, their governess could not wait to have them back again.

During the earliest years of her infancy, Princess Margaret was not often seen – or perhaps, more correctly, not often noticed – by the general public. As a result, a story was invented that she was being withheld from public view because she was both deaf and dumb. The perpetrators of such stories – and their motives – are forever unknown; but it seems that, unless royal progeny are thrust into the limelight almost as soon as they draw breath, stories are liable to circulate that they are in some way abnormal. Admittedly there have been royal children whose health has given cause for concern, and thus the need for special protection, but Princess Margaret was not one of them. 'Mama thought me rather chatty,' the Princess herself has said.

Among those who could laugh at the absurdity of such a rumour was Sir James Barrie, the creator of Peter Pan. After he had attended one of Princess Margaret's earliest parties (the Princess believes it was to mark her fifth birthday), Sir James noted:

> Some of her presents were on the table, simple things that might have come from the sixpenny shops, but she was in a frenzy of glee over them, especially one to which she had given the place of honour by her plate. I said to her as one astounded, 'Is that really your very own?' and she saw how I envied and immediately placed it between us with the words, 'It is yours and mine.'

Kindliness and humility were prominent among Princess Margaret's characteristics. Never for one moment was she allowed to believe herself a cut above the rest. In her own words, 'I would have been teased dreadfully if I had. I was probably thought a horrid child anyway.' Simplicity of thought was always encouraged, particularly by the three women who, together with her sister, helped more than anyone else to influence the Princess's formative years. They were her mother, her nanny and her governess.

The formal education of the two Princesses was catered for in a set programme of lessons devised by Miss Crawford. Half an hour's religious instruction began the week at 9.30 every Monday morning. Subsequent mornings always began with an arithmetic lesson, followed by history, grammar, geography, literature or writing. Mme Montaudon-Smith taught French, while Mlle Georgina Guérin gave them French conversation during the holidays. After three lessons of half an hour each, there was a break between eleven and twelve o'clock for the Princesses to take a drink of orange juice and play games in Hamilton Gardens. They then had an hour's rest, during which they read silently to themselves or Crawfie read aloud to them. After lunch, on Mondays Miss Betty Vacani taught dancing, on Tuesdays they attended singing classes at the Knightsbridge home of the Countess of Cavan, on Wednesdays they were taught drawing, on Thursdays there was a music lesson, and on Friday afternoon the family generally left for Royal Lodge, Windsor Great Park. On Saturday mornings, from half past nine until eleven o'clock, the Princesses did a résumé of the week's work and some general reading. This was followed by an hour's riding and then, after lunch, they spent the afternoon with their parents.

Today Princess Margaret's recollections of life at 145 Piccadilly are rather vague. Her memories of life at Royal Lodge, however, and of some of her parents more distinguished visitors are more distinct. One guest she remembers with particular clarity was the Archbishop of Canterbury, Dr Cosmo Gordon Lang, who invariably managed to embarrass her by placing his hand firmly on her head and solemnly declaring, 'Bless you, my child.'

As a toddler, the sight of her 'small fat face' – as her governess put it – peering slowly round the door of her parents' dining-room was guaranteed to delight. Moments later she would be perched on her father's knee, sipping 'windy water' (a Scottish expression for soda water), crunching brown sugar crystals or graphically describing what the Duke called the 'hooshmi' – any spoon-fed mixture – that had been served for her own meal.

Even at an early age Princess Margaret had a keen sense of the theatrical. A particular childhood pleasure was to be taken to the pantomime each Christmas and afterwards to re-enact with her family what she had seen on stage. Years later it was to be said that, had fate not placed her apart from the rest of society, she could easily have followed an acting career. This was not true and the Princess knew it. In fact, she developed very early on a finely-tuned ear for an empty or sycophantic compliment. All the same, as proof of a musical bent, Lady Strathmore testified to hearing her granddaughter – at the age of nine months – hum the waltz from *The Merry Widow* as she was carried down from the nursery at Glamis. 'I was so astounded', the Countess told Lady Cynthia Asquith, 'that I almost dropped her.' And at the age of three, as one of the Princess's cousins recalls, she could sing all the words of the hymn *There is a Green Hill Far Away*.

The Princess was certainly an imaginative child and from her inventive mind sprang two childhood companions, the first of whom was 'Cousin Halifax'. For her there was always time for a chat, even at the most inopportune moments. 'I was talking to Cousin Halifax,' she would reply airily if interrupted by a summons back to reality. Indispensable though Cousin Halifax was, she always took second place to another character by the name of 'Inderbombanks'. Of indeterminate sex – 'I suppose he must have been male,' says the Princess – he became her parents' favourite and while, in later years, Cousin Halifax had slipped her creator's mind, Inderbombanks was never to be forgotten.

Recreation had, of course, been given a time and place in the

Princesses well-ordered day. Yet even while they played their games in Hamilton Gardens, good behaviour could never quite be forgotten. As with most enclosed gardens of this type in London, that which was associated with the tall houses of Piccadilly, although private, was not exclusive to any one family. Furthermore, the garden's open railings were inviting to strangers, who invariably gathered there each day to watch the King's granddaughters at play. It was something to which neither Princess ever became accustomed.

Nonetheless, with or without staring faces, the sisters threw themselves wholeheartedly into their games. Hide-and-seek (or variations of it) was a game they particularly enjoyed. Like Cowboys and Indians it was something in which their governess could also take part. Then there were races to and from Lord Byron's statue nearby and sometimes the Duke of York would enthusiastically join in his daughters' games of hopscotch.

On wet or cold afternoons there were less boisterous pursuits at number 145. There were stories to be told (one of Princess Margaret's early favourites was *The Little Red Hen*, which she was said to know so well she could almost recite it by heart); and books to be read like A. A. Milne's *Winnie the Pooh*, *Lamb's Tales from Shakespeare* and Thackeray's *The Rose and the Ring*. The Princesses' fondness for horses was already keenly developed, and from time to time horse markets would be organized beneath the glass-domed roof on the top floor of the house. Here was kept their considerable collection of toy horses, which had to be groomed, fed and watered 'all day' as Princess Margaret recalls. Pretending to be horses was also a favourite game and, when not playing in an imaginary ship among the rhododendron bushes in the grounds of Royal Lodge, the Princesses would take it in turns to put on a jangling harness and pull one another round the garden paths. Later, when they were old enough, Mr Owen, a groom at Windsor, taught the Princesses to ride.

On a more practical level, both children had their own small gardens to tend at Royal Lodge. In hers Princess Elizabeth chose to grow flowers, while Princess Margaret grew potatoes – 'King Edward's', she declared, 'were the best.'

Housework was another playtime activity. At 145 Piccadilly the Princesses were taught to clean and help out in the nursery pantry, while at Windsor there was the thatched cottage called *Y Bwthyn Bach–To Gwellt* (The Little House with the Straw Roof) to be kept clean and tidy. This cottage, a scaled down version in every detail of a full-sized house, had been presented to Princess Elizabeth by the people of Wales and was in turn to be a great attraction for the royal children of the next generation when staying at Windsor. Today, its custodian is Princess Margaret's daughter, Lady Sarah Armstrong-Jones.

To the outsider – and it is as true nowadays as it was then – the lives of royalty appear more exceptional than they really are. 'I am only a very ordinary person when people let me be one,' the Duke of York once said, and it is the kind of remark that might easily have been made by either of his daughters. Royal figures are often thought to inhabit a completely different world and are expected to behave differently, and better, than other people; the public distances them in a mood of 'them and us'. Certainly if the Duke and Duchess of York never ceased to be astounded by the interest their daughters generated, it was because they saw in other children the very same unremarkable behaviour of both Princesses.

From their earliest days the Princesses developed a great bond of love and friendship, though this could not help but give way to a certain amount of rivalry which occasionally ended in a fight. Deliberate provocation, like Princess Margaret plucking the elastic of her sister's hat (or vice versa), was sure to guarantee battle stations. At such times Princess Elizabeth would pinch and Princess Margaret, as the smaller, would retaliate with a kick. 'I never won,' she remembers.

The Silver Jubilee of the reign of King George v brought royal pageantry into Princess Margaret's life long before she could fully understand what it represented to the British people.

To the granddaughters he adored, but more especially to Princess Margaret, the old King was a gruff, shadowy figure, an impression created by Allah's own fear of him, and it was precisely this fear that resulted in Allah's infrequent visits to Buckingham Palace with the Princesses. Ironically, however, it was not so much the King as Queen Mary, ever a formidable figure in their lives, who tended to intimidate, for in much the same way that the Queen was incapable of close communication with her own children, so was she unable to reach her granddaughters. Furthermore, while she felt quite at home in male company, she was always decidedly ill at ease with her own sex. The inevitable distance that resulted instilled a fear of her in both Princesses.

'Whenever we had to visit Granny at Marlborough House,' Princess Margaret recalls, 'we always felt that we were going to be hauled over the coals for something we had done. But we never were.' Nonetheless, this childhood impression never left them and, even today, both the Queen and Princess Margaret can recall 'the hollow, empty feeling' they had in the pit of their stomachs whenever their grandmother sent for them.

The celebration of the Silver Jubilee of their grandparents' reign was the first big royal spectacle in which the Princesses participated, though Princess Margaret has no recollection of the event. They had both been present at Westminster Abbey in November 1934 for the wedding of their uncle the Duke of Kent to Princess Marina of Greece, but a younger son's marriage could in no way be compared to the celebration of the sovereign's jubilee.

The day for the official service of thanksgiving at St Paul's Cathedral was set for Monday 6 May 1935, a portentous date in royal history books. Twenty-five years earlier on 6 May 1910, the King's father, Edward VII, had died, and on 6 May 1960, precisely twenty-five years after her grandfather's jubilee, Princess Margaret was married. Like the day of the Princess's wedding, 6 May 1935 was, to quote Queen Mary, 'a lovely, warm day'. Street decorations gave London a very festive air, matched only by the good humour of all those lining the route of the royal procession to St Paul's. 'Crowds in the parks and streets quite early,' the Queen noted in her diary.

At 10 a.m. the Royal Family set out in their carriages from Buckingham Palace. Seated with their parents in one of the maroon and gold state landaus were the Princesses Elizabeth and Margaret, 'two tiny pink children', as diarist Sir Henry ('Chips') Channon observed.

At the close of that day, having broadcast to his peoples across the empire, a contented and emotional George V noted in his journal, 'I'd no idea they felt like that about me. I am beginning to think they must really like me for myself.' If it was true – and it almost certainly was – that the King had not been able to fathom the depth of his subjects' feelings towards him before the jubilee, then, at least in retrospect, the event must surely have been touched with pathos.

George V died eight months later at the start of what history has called 'the year of the three Kings'. On the death of his father on 20 January 1936, the Prince of Wales was proclaimed 'His Most Excellent Majesty, Edward the Eighth'. Ten months later, at the height of the greatest constitutional crisis of the century, his brother, the Duke of York, ascended the throne as King George VI. For the Duke and Duchess of York, Edward VIII's decision was the realization of their worst fears; fears which had grown appreciably as Prince Edward's determination to marry Mrs Simpson gathered momentum.

Of the events that led so rapidly to the abdication of her uncle and the accession of her father, Princess Margaret knew little. She grasped of the situation only what her sister was able to tell her. Nevertheless, she understood the implications of her family's imminent change in status when Princess Elizabeth told her, 'Uncle David is going away and isn't coming back, and Papa is to be King.'

Wide-eyed, Princess Margaret asked, 'Does that mean you are going to be *Queen*?' For a six-year-old it was an awe-inspiring thought.

Precisely what did Edward VIII's departure mean to the young Princess Margaret? The short answer is: not a great deal. Many stories have been told of the devotion felt by Edward for his 'favourite nieces' – until 25 December 1936, when Princess Alexandra of Kent was born, two weeks after the Duke of Windsor had left Britain for France, the Princesses Elizabeth and Margaret were his *only* nieces – but such stories, in common with others which spoke of the myriad games he loved to play with them, are apocryphal. As Princess Margaret herself says, 'We didn't know him.' Nor for that matter did the nation know him as well as it may have thought.

In an essay written after the former King had married Wallis Warfield Simpson, Virginia Woolf summed up the feelings of many people. Dukes and princes, she wrote, had said they were no longer going to play the game – one had married a Smith* and another a Simpson: 'We said we cannot dream our dreams about people with

---

* It is probable that Virginia Woolf was referring to (Sir) Henry Abel Smith who, in 1931, married the Lady May Cambridge (formerly Princess May of Teck), the only daughter of Princess Alice, Countess of Athlone, and the Earl of Athlone (formerly Prince Alexander of Teck, a brother of Queen Mary).

hearts like ours. Such names as Smith and Simpson rouse us to reality.'

The final act of Edward VIII as King was to sign the Instrument of Abdication. This he did in his ground-floor study at Fort Belvedere at 10 a.m. on the morning of Thursday 10 December 1936. As the document was signed, the Duke of Cornwall's flag which, even as King he chose to fly, was lowered. It was a symbolic gesture in recognition of the transfer of monarchical responsibilities. As soon as the document had been signed and witnessed by the departing sovereign, his successor and the Dukes of Gloucester and Kent, the flag was raised again. The actual Act of Abdication, 'A Bill to give effect to His Majesty's declaration ...', was signed on the following day.

With her sons gathered at Fort Belvedere, Queen Mary drove to 145 Piccadilly to visit the new Queen. When she left, one contemporary newspaper report told its readers: 'Many of the women ... were crying and two old and shabbily-dressed men stood bareheaded in the frosty air.' Also watching their grandmother leave were the two Princesses. When they were spotted at an upper window of the house, they withdrew into the room, pulling a heavy curtain across the window after them.

From the moment her uncle signed the abdication papers, Princess Elizabeth became heiress presumptive to her father's throne and Princess Margaret stepped up one place in the line of succession. A sovereign's daughter needs no surname and the Princess, who had only just learned to write her full name, said sadly to a friend, 'I used to be Margaret of York and now I'm nothing.'

King George VI ascended the throne four days before his forty-first birthday. Apart from his brother, he was the youngest prince to become king since George III in 1760 at the age of twenty-two. For the past thirteen years he had been a happily married man, at his most content at home with his wife and daughters. His innate modesty, marked to some degree by a feeling of inferiority stemming from the tactics of a heavy-handed childhood, and exacerbated by his stammer, prevented him from harbouring high-flown ambitions. He had, however, a strong sense of duty and it was this, bolstered by the encouragement of his wife, that led him to fulfil his royal role – one which he never found easy – with a quiet but indisputable success.

'I went to see Queen Mary,' he confided to his diary concerning his brother's decision to abdicate, '& when I told her what had happened I broke down & sobbed like a child.' Later, while his wife and confidante was confined to bed with influenza, the new King turned to his cousin, Lord Louis Mountbatten (Earl Mountbatten of Burma). 'Dickie, this is absolutely terrible,' he exclaimed. 'I never wanted this to happen; I'm quite unprepared for it. David has been trained for this all his life.... I'm only a Naval Officer, it's the only thing I know about.'

Mountbatten replied, 'This is a very curious coincidence. My father once told me that, when the Duke of Clarence [George v's elder brother] died, your father came to him and said almost the same things that you have said to me now, and my father answered: "George, you're wrong. There is no more fitting preparation for a King than to have been trained in the Navy."'

King George VI and Queen Elizabeth were not a glamorous couple, nor were they expected to be. The prevailing circumstances demanded not a dashing life-style like that of Edward VIII, but a renewed dedication to both the Crown and the empire. The new King and Queen provided stability and the nation loved them for it.

Lord Mountbatten later paid tribute to King George VI during a private conversation he had with Princess Margaret after the King's death in 1952. 'Your father,' Mountbatten said, 'was made of integrity, and that was something your Uncle David never had. *That* is why your father was such a smashing success as King.'

CHAPTER THREE

THE KING'S DAUGHTER

The new Royal Family vacated 145 Piccadilly in two deliberately planned stages. First King George and Queen Elizabeth moved to Buckingham Palace, which the King had inherited with as much reluctance as his crown. However, as the official London residence of the sovereign, it had to be accepted with the job. To the Princesses the Palace was virtually unknown territory. They had, of course, been taken there on private visits and on such ceremonial occasions as their grandfather's Silver Jubilee, but it had never been a place in which they could wander where they pleased. All that would now change.

Once the King and Queen were installed at the Palace, the second stage of the move was to introduce the Princesses to their new home. In order that they might adjust more naturally to their grander surroundings, their parents arranged for them to be brought across from Piccadilly on a series of regular visits. In this way it was hoped that the transition from visitors to residents would be accomplished with fewer anxieties. Before they formally moved in – on 17 February 1937 – the Princesses would have time to become acclimatized to the idea of seeing their parents 'at home'. One advantage of the move was that the Princesses would now have ample opportunities to play outside without an eager crowd of onlookers, for they had what amounted to their very own private garden.

Vast though Buckingham Palace is, it was never a daunting place in which to live. It is true that Edward VII had not liked it at all, nor for that matter had Edward VIII, but both Queen Alexandra and her daughter-in-law, Queen Mary, became very attached to it. 'Those lovely comfortable rooms which have been my happy home ...,' Queen Mary said nostalgically when, as Queen Dowager, she had had to move to Marlborough House following her husband's death. Buckingham Palace is certainly not the cavernous museum it is sometimes imagined to be.

The royal apartments – that is to say the private suite – occupy part of the first floor, overlooking Green Park in one direction and the garden in the other. On the floor above were the nurseries. Here the Princesses would live, high enough to see over the Victoria Memorial and along the Mall, and an admirable spot from which to view the Changing of the Guard each morning in the forecourt below.

Princess Margaret's lasting impression of her family's move is not one of trepidation; in fact quite the reverse. She remembers 'battling through enormous, loving crowds' as her family approached the Palace gates. Both Princess Margaret and her sister adapted well and effortlessly to their new surroundings. Together they explored the long corridors of the nursery floor, the younger Princess riding her kiddy-car (a type of tricycle), and the well-worn cry, 'Wait for me Lilibet, wait for *me*,' became a familiar sound to members of their parents' household. 'It was as though the place had been dead for years and had suddenly come alive,' said one member of staff.

In selecting a new schoolroom for the Princesses, Miss Crawford was accompanied on a tour of the Palace by the King. Remembering the gloomy schoolroom of his own childhood, associated with disagreeable memories of his tutor, the King wanted to avoid a similar forbidding environment for his daughters. A bright room overlooking the garden and the lake was chosen. Here Princess Elizabeth and Princess Margaret would follow their separate lessons with their governess, pursuing uninterrupted the routine that had been established at 145 Piccadilly.

For the King and Queen this settling in period was increasingly dominated by arrangements for the impending coronation, now less than three months away. In normal circumstances, a period of about a year to eighteen months separates a sovereign's accession and coronation, but the circumstances of George VI's inheritance were far from normal and it was considered inexpedient to alter the date that had already been set for Edward VIII's crowning – Wednesday 12 May.

The coronation of her parents was the first great occasion that Princess Margaret is able to recall with any degree of clarity. For the Princesses it was to prove a long day, but one that presented a spectacle of solemn ritual, magnificent theatre and carnival-like jubilation. The elder Princess had just celebrated her eleventh birthday, the younger was not yet seven. While Princess Elizabeth felt quite grown-up enough to take the ordeal in her stride, she did wonder whether or not her sister was quite ready for so awesome an occasion: 'She is very young for a coronation, isn't she?' she remarked in concern.

The day began unwelcomingly early for the King and Queen – at three in the morning – for at that otherwise unearthly hour Ministry of Works engineers began testing loudspeakers erected along Constitution Hill. 'One of them might have been in our room,' noted the King.

Throughout their childhood both Princesses had always been dressed alike and the coronation was no exception. Their dresses were of white lace, adorned with silver bows. On their heads they wore light-weight coronets specially fashioned by order of the King, and from their shoulders fell trains of purple velvet trimmed with ermine. Only on this point was there a minor *contretemps*. Princess Margaret's train was a little shorter than her sister's and she wanted to know why. The answer had nothing to do with rank, as some have implied in the past. It was simply that the mantles were designed and cut in proportion to the Princesses' height. Once this had been explained, Princess Margaret complained no more.

From Buckingham Palace the two Princesses set out in the Irish State Coach, accompanied by their aunt Mary, the Princess Royal, and her son George, Viscount Lascelles (now Earl of Harewood). Upon their arrival at Westminster Abbey, they made their way through the Royal Entrance and into the nave. There, preceded by Rouge Croix Pursuivant and Rouge Dragon Pursuivant and two gentlemen ushers, the Princesses led the procession of British royalty to the Royal Gallery. Behind them walked the Duchesses of Gloucester and Kent, Prince and Princess Arthur of Connaught, Princess Alice, Countess of Athlone (who, in preparation for the coronation of the present Queen in 1953, taught the ladies-in-waiting how to fold the long velvet trains correctly), Lady Patricia Ramsay and the Princesses Helena Victoria and Marie Louise.

Queen Mary, a stately figure with her long mantle supported by four page-boys, then processed through the abbey with her sister-in-law, Queen Maud of Norway, to take her position in the Royal Gallery next to Princess Margaret. With the arrival of the King and Queen, the lengthy ceremony finally commenced.

One detail in all the meticulous planning had been overlooked, however. Nobody had thought to explain fully to the youngest member of the congregation the step-by-step significance of the service. Consequently Princess Margaret peered down on a glittering scene that left her somewhat bemused. A glance now and then at her grandmother and the Princess Royal – both of whom were preoccupied with their tears – told her that no explanation would be forthcoming from either direction, so the little Princess remained silent and waited patiently until the ceremony came to an end.

As the royal processions wound their way back to Buckingham Palace, all London – or so it seemed – erupted in a cacophony of sound. And it was for precisely this reason that a machine had been wired up on a roof somewhere in Whitehall: a decibel counter. As the state carriages faded into the distant throng of Trafalgar Square, it was estimated that the King and Queen had elicited cheers registering eighty-three decibels, while the Princesses, now driving with Queen Mary in the Queen Alexandra State Coach, had elicited eighty-five decibels.

Within hours of the coronation's completion reports of the ceremony were being transmitted around the world. Amongst all the gushing platitudes and glowing descriptions of Britain's day of glory, one small item which has often been repeated irked the young Princess Margaret. She had, according to one American newspaper, 'riffled the pages of her prayer book' during the ceremony. 'I did not!' she later protested. 'I wouldn't have dared ... I was sitting *between* Granny and Aunt Mary!'

At the end of the day both the King and his elder daughter picked up their pens to record their feelings about the events of the day. For Princess Elizabeth one of the most memorable moments had been when the peeresses lifted their long, white-gloved arms to place their coronets on their heads. 'They looked like swans,' she noted. While Princess Elizabeth wrote her essay in a mood of elation, describing how 'the abbey came to life once more', her father opened his diary to leave posterity with a note of what had not gone quite according to plan:

> After the Introduction I removed my Parliamentary robes ... and moved to the Coronation chair. Here various vestments were placed upon me, the white Colobium Sindonis, a surplice which the Dean of Westminster insisted I should put on inside out, had not my Groom of the Robes come to the rescue. Before this I knelt at the Altar to take the Coronation Oath. I had two Bishops, Durham and Wells, one on either side to support me & to hold the form of Service for me to follow. When this great moment came neither Bishop could find the words, so the Archbishop held his book down for me to read, but horror of horrors his thumb covered the words of the Oath.

More was to come: the Lord Great Chamberlain shook so much that the King had to fasten his sword-belt personally, St Edward's Crown was very nearly put on the King's head the wrong way round, and one of the attendant bishops trod on His Majesty's robes, almost pulling him down. 'I had to tell him to get off it pretty sharply,' wrote the King, to the subsequent amusement of his family.

In King George's eyes his daughters were both 'wonderful and strange'. They seemed to accomplish with ease so much which had been a torment to him. They learned to swim in a public pool with other children and they were able to mix in a way that had never been allowed when he was a boy.

Happy though Princess Margaret and her sister were in each other's company, they realized very early the inevitable restrictions which their positions imposed. For example, to watch from a distance other children at play was to be reminded that others' lives were unfettered by the red tape and ceremony that is so much a part of a royal existence. This is not to say, however, that the Princesses felt in any way deprived. They did not. Indeed both of them remember the years of their childhood as 'idyllic'. Furthermore, there were enough children of their own age group in and around the Royal Family generally from whom to choose friends and companions. Of them all, Princess Margaret felt particularly close to the children of her aunt, Lady Elphinstone. With them, she and Princess Elizabeth would march across the drive at Birkhall on the Balmoral estate singing at the tops of their voices; they would spend days fishing together or having picnics at the edge of Loch Muick or beside the small cottages beloved of Queen Victoria, who referred to Balmoral as 'This Dear Paradise'.

Children from outside the royal circle also crossed the Princesses' paths. During the war years there were evacuees lodged on the royal estates and, nearer the Princesses' social background, there were the girls who were enlisted into the Buckingham Palace Girl Guide Company and Brownie Pack, which had been formed at Queen Elizabeth's instigation shortly after the family moved to Buckingham Palace. As the elder, Princess Elizabeth joined the Kingfisher Patrol of the Girl Guides, while Princess Margaret joined the Leprechaun Six of the Brownies and later graduated to the Bullfinch Patrol of the Guides, when she earned her proficiency badges in such subjects as morse code, first aid and cooking, and was finally awarded the much coveted 'All-round Cords'. In the war, the Princesses continued their guide activities at Windsor, joined by Cockney evacuees to the royal estate, and turned their hands to knitting comforters for the troops, rolling bandages and collecting tin foil and the Sphagnum moss that was used for surgical dressings.

As with most undertakings of their daughters, the King and Queen proved enthusiastic, even indulgent, in their support. King George was happy to approve everything about the idea of the Princesses joining the Guides and Brownies – except part of their uniform. 'I'll stand anything,' he said, 'but I won't have them wear those hideous long black stockings. Reminds me too much of my youth.'

There was certainly little reason for George VI to remember his early years with affection. The regime that had occupied his days was strict almost to the point of being loveless. At least in retrospect, there was something surprisingly soulless about the way in which his parents entrusted their offspring to a regiment of servants who were encouraged to enforce a harsh discipline that in fact sometimes amounted to cruelty. Nevertheless the Prince gave his love to his parents and more spontaneously to his elder brother and his only sister, Princess Mary, between whom he stood, like pig-in-the-middle, trying to gain at least a small share of parental attention and approval.

In his memoirs, *A King's Story*, The Duke of Windsor wrote, 'I have often felt that despite his undoubted affection for all of us, my father preferred children in the abstract, and that his notion of a small boy's place in a grown-up world was summed up in the phrase, "Children should be seen, not heard".' So distant a father was King George V, in fact, that Princess Alice, Countess of Athlone, one of the few members of the Royal Family who did not stand in fear of him, once asked outright, 'George, don't you love your children?'

'Of *course* I do!' the King snapped.

'Then why don't you *show* it?' the Princess retorted with equal force.

Despite what he had endured as a child and the considerable strain he felt in coping with his royal role – occasionally demonstrated in a fleeting burst of temper – King George VI is remembered by his family as a light-hearted, amusing man; his fun-loving and kindly nature remains foremost in their memories.

In contrast, the overall impression of Queen Elizabeth's childhood is one of supreme happiness. The Strathmores, more a clan than a family, never aspired to social greatness. Lord Strathmore's wife, Cecilia, freer by far to speak her mind than most women of her day, was a sensible, devoutly religious, firm but loving wife and parent. These qualities, admired in the mother, were clearly apparent in her youngest daughter, Elizabeth.

Constance Smith, a great friend of the Strathmores, provides an idea of Cecilia's character in an extract from her journal: ' "The Duke of Leeds is a wise man," Lord Strathmore said. "Why?" said I. "Why? – well, he yachts a good deal – and he shoots – and then he hunts – and enjoys himself." "Wise," says Cecilia firmly, "do you call *that* wise?" '

A similar exchange today might well elicit the same sort of no-nonsense reply from Queen Elizabeth the Queen Mother, and probably from her daughter too, for Princess Margaret shares the directness of manner characteristic of both her mother and maternal grandmother.

During the closing years of the 1930s, the threat of another war was constantly in the background and by 1939 most people accepted that it was an imminent reality. The role of the Royal Family in maintaining morale was clearly going to be important, and to put particular strain on King George VI and Queen Elizabeth.

Less than two months before Britain issued her ultimatum to Germany in September 1939, the King expressed a wish to inspect the Royal Naval College at Dartmouth. The suggestion was prompted less by curiosity on the part of one of the college's most famous old boys than by the sovereign's earnest desire to see how the cadets of his Navy were shaping up at a particularly crucial time. The King was accompanied by Queen Elizabeth, the two Princesses and Lord Louis Mountbatten.

At the end of the visit, as the old royal yacht the *Victoria and Albert* steamed out of Dartmouth Harbour, it left behind a saluting flotilla of 109 small boats. Only the one hundred and tenth continued in pursuit: an insignificant craft, pitching and rolling in the wake of the yacht. The lone oarsman's act of bravado was watched by the Royal Family with considerable consternation. 'The damned young fool!' barked the King. And it was only when Lord Mountbatten's bellowed command to return to base reached his ears that Cadet Captain H.R.H. Prince Philip of Greece obeyed.

The Royal Family's visit to Dartmouth that July achieved fame if for no other reason than it was the occasion on which Princess Elizabeth, then aged thirteen, first met her future husband. It was also the first time that the nine-year-old Princess Margaret met the man with whom, so some have claimed, she was destined to embark on a precariously balanced, if not barbed, relationship. Princess Margaret, on the other hand, asserts that she has always shared 'a genial relationship' with Prince Philip.

War was finally declared on 3 September, little more than a month after the Royal Family had begun its annual highland holiday at Birkhall. The steadily declining political situation had already caused a delay in their departure – at which Princess Margaret had asked indignantly, 'Who *is* this Hitler, spoiling everything?' – and now the King and Queen had to return to London with all speed. The Princesses were to remain in the safety of Deeside until further notice.

They in fact stayed on at Birkhall until December; this would in itself have been a novel experience for them both even if the cowman had not caught diphtheria, so that everybody had to be innoculated, the Princesses could not attend Girl Guide meetings, and the nativity play in which they were to appear had to be cancelled. Novelty, however, soon gave way to the established routine of lessons, private study and recreation.

Breaks – or rather pauses – occurred from time to time, as when the Princesses helped to serve tea following sewing parties held at Birkhall as part of the war effort. In addition there were evacuees to be met, children from the Glasgow slums who, by order of the King, were accommodated at Craigowan House on the royal estate. The evacuees arrived from the village hall, where they had been cleaned and de-loused. Sadly, most of the children were unable to adjust to their new surroundings: the royal estates were an alien world to them and at night the wind groaning through the trees terrified them. It was, they said, the sound of witches and devils.

For Princess Elizabeth and Princess Margaret, the first frosts brought laughter at the discovery of frozen water in the ewers, frozen sponges and frozen face flannels. Sometimes, when a local film enthusiast was invited to the house, there were gales of fresh laughter at the antics of Charlie Chaplin and the Keystone Cops.

In the same way that the Princesses never considered their lives exceptional or outstanding before the outbreak of war, so there was nothing particularly remarkable about their lives as evacuees, save that they were only ever 'evacuated' to their own houses. It was in October 1939 that the effects of war reached them in the Highlands. The first jolt came that month when the battleship *Royal Oak* was torpedoed by a German U-boat which had penetrated the Scapa Flow defences. The news that the British ship had sunk with the loss of all hands greatly saddened the Princesses.

Another reminder of war was the voice of William Joyce, better known as 'Lord Haw-Haw', whose menacing tones always seemed to be heard whenever the wireless was switched on. To save the set from probable destruction it was usually turned off again without delay for the Princesses would reach for books, cushions and any other handy missiles with which to bombard the source of the offending voice.

However, the war was brought home in a very personal and painful way to the Royal Family when, in August 1942, the King's younger brother, Prince George, Duke of Kent, was killed on active service when his plane crashed over Scotland. 'I came down to breakfast to be given the news by my sister,' Princess Margaret remembers. 'The entire family was devastated ... we adored him.'

As the first Christmas of the war approached and the Princesses were taken into Aberdeen to shop for gifts – small trinkets and such like – the question they asked was where they would be spending the holidays. For a time the answer hung in the balance. Then, one evening during the daily telephone conversations she and the King had with their daughters, the Queen was able to give them the good news that Christmas would be spent at Sandringham near King's Lynn in Norfolk, despite its dangerous proximity to one of the stretches of coast thought most likely to suffer an invasion.

On Christmas Eve, as was the custom, the lights on the tall pine tree in the drawing-room at Sandringham House were lit and gifts were exchanged. Among those the Princesses received from their mother were their first diaries. For King George vi, however, the festive season only began after he had delivered his Christmas message to the peoples of the Empire. Of public speaking he had always said, 'This is an ordeal,' and so it was. The thought that he might suddenly stammer or dry up in mid-sentence always haunted him, a dread that was only made less terrifying on his last broadcast, when his speech was pre-recorded; before that royal transmissions went out live.

The King's message of hope that year was eventually to become his epitaph. Shortly before his speech was completed, he received a copy of a poem entitled 'The Gate of the Year'. It had been written by Miss Marie Louise (Minnie) Haskins, a lecturer at the London School of Economics, who had published it privately in 1908 as part of a collection entitled *The Desert*:

> I said to the man who stood at the Gate of the Year,
> 'Give me a light so that I may tread safely into the unknown,'
> And he replied, 'Go out into the darkness,
> And put your hand into the Hand of God.
> That shall be to you better than light,
> And safer than a known way.'

Princess Margaret and her sister remained at Sandringham until February 1940, when they moved to Royal Lodge, Windsor Great Park. Due to cautious censorship of information, they were officially described as living 'somewhere in the country'. Windsor, directly beneath the flight path of enemy aircraft following the Thames to London, was by no means as safe as Balmoral. In time the Princesses could identify the bombers by the sounds they made: 'ours' or 'theirs' they would say. The greatest benefit of this move was that it reunited the Princesses with their parents who, unless taken further afield by duty, commuted to and from London each day by car.

Queen Mary had viewed plans for her own evacuation to Badminton House, the home of her niece, the Duchess of Beaufort, and her husband, with little enthusiasm. To leave London at such a time she had said, was not 'at all the thing'. King George VI, however, persuaded her that if she stayed, her presence would only cause added anxiety. The dowager Queen acquiesced and moved to the West Country, taking with her the majority of her staff and their dependants, numbering well over sixty in all.

In Scotland the Princesses had, for the most part, been insulated against the war and, though to a lesser degree, the same was true of their stay at Royal Lodge. However, when in May 1940 enemy forces invaded Holland, Belgium and Luxembourg, Britain seemed no more than a goose-step away. It was then that the order was given: the King's daughters must leave Royal Lodge for Windsor Castle.

CHAPTER FOUR

WARTIME MANOEUVRES

In the event of an invasion, plans had been made to evacuate the Royal Family to Canada, via Liverpool. When this contingency was first discussed, neither King George VI nor Queen Elizabeth were in favour of leaving Britain, even if faced by the most dangerous of situations. 'The children could not leave without me,' said the Queen emphatically, 'I could not leave without the King, and the King will never leave.' Indeed it has been said that the sovereign himself was ready to lead a resistance movement should enemy forces have set foot in his kingdom.

In May 1940, however, moving the Princesses to Windsor Castle was regarded as a temporary measure, expected to last no more than a week. In the end they stayed until hostilities ceased five years later. Although the castle was no longer the impenetrable fortress it had once been, it still afforded far greater facilities for the Princesses' safety than Royal Lodge, its distinctive pink walls now washed with the murky colours of camouflage.

At this time Windsor Castle may have seemed to some a gloomy cavern of a place with its treasures removed into safe-keeping, daylight filtering through windows covered by wire netting to prevent flying glass, reduced electric lighting and thick black-out curtains. But all this was accepted without a second thought by the King's daughters and, although one senior-ranking member of the household likened the atmosphere to that of a convent, Princess Margaret talks of the great esprit de corps she remembers. 'There was a tremendous spirit at Windsor,' she says, 'everybody was always cheerful.'

The nightly passage of the Luftwaffe is something else the Princess recalls: enemy aircraft 'always seemed to come over when we had just got to sleep'. At such times the 'red alert' was given and the Princesses were roused from their beds. Siren suits were hastily zipped up and, clutching small suitcases containing their most important possessions, they made their way along subterranean passages, smelling 'disgustingly damp', to their shelter. Sleep, however, was usually out of the question, which meant that the Princesses were scarcely able to keep their eyes open during lessons the following day. To remedy the situation a 'concrete box', as the Princess described it, was erected beneath one of the towers. This new 'apartment', complete with every necessary facility including proper beds, was where the Princesses spent their nights, virtually undisturbed, until the war's end.

Three days after the royal party took up residence, a company of Grenadiers, detailed to the King's protection, arrived. The castle grounds were heavily scored with trenches and barbed wire fences which 'wouldn't have kept anybody out, but kept us in'; and in case the Princesses found themselves isolated while out in the park during a daytime raid, an armoured car stood ready to collect them.

There were scares, of course, as when a German VI missile roared over the royal estate one afternoon. Directly beneath it Princess Margaret and her fellow Girl Guides were setting up camp. At its approach they flung themselves to the ground and lay there motionless until it had passed. Clearing the Home Park and the castle itself, the 'doodle-bug' cut out a few minutes later and dropped from the sky over the Maidenhead road. Narrowly missing Windsor racecourse, where a heavily-attended meeting was in progress, it decimated a nearby house, instantly claiming the life of its owner.

Four months later, at her own suggestion, Princess Elizabeth spoke to the children of the empire. In her five-minute broadcast, transmitted by the B.B.C. on 13 October, during *Children's Hour*, the Princess told her listeners: 'I can truthfully say to you all that we children at home are full of cheerfulness and courage. We are trying to do all we can to help our gallant sailors, soldiers and airmen, and we are trying, too, to bear our own share of the danger and sadness of war. We know, every one of us, that in the end all will be well.'

As she spoke, Princess Margaret sat nervously beside her, waiting for her promised cue. It came when Princess Elizabeth said, 'My sister is by my side, and we are both going to say goodnight to you. Come on, Margaret.' 'Goodnight and good luck to you all,' the Princess joined in. At that moment it is said that even the enormously strong reserve of Queen Mary weakened and she allowed herself the luxury of a few tears.

Less exciting was the daily routine of the two Princesses, which continued to follow the same pattern it always had, despite their moves from London to Birkhall, Birkhall to Sandringham and Sandringham to Windsor. Luncheon each day did provide some slight variation, however, with the practice of inviting two officers of the Grenadier Guards to join them. As one officer testified, both Princesses became very popular with the entire company

Even at that age Princess Margaret's wit was devilish enough to amuse or intimidate. 'If you sat at Princess Margaret's end of the table,' remarked one young officer, 'the conversation never lapsed for a moment. She was amazingly self-assured, without being embarrassingly so.'

A year or two later, Queen Mary confided to Mabell, Countess of Airlie, a close friend and lady-in-waiting, that Princess Margaret was 'so outrageously amusing that one can't help encouraging her'. She was '*espiègle*' – a mischievous little rogue.

To the King himself, Princess Margaret seemed to possess natural qualities which could dispel an awkward moment or cheer him if crestfallen. 'In Princess Elizabeth', explained Sir John Wheeler-Bennett, 'King George saw certain of his own traits; his own combination of humour and dignity, his common sense and eagle eye for detail.' In Princess Margaret was 'the same quick mind and with it a vivacious charm, a sparkling sense of wit, an appreciation of the ludicrous. She it was who could always make her father laugh, even when he was angry with her.'

Guaranteed to appeal to the King's sense of fun – although he may never have read it – was a specimen 'thank you' letter written by Princess Margaret as part of an exercise to win her Girl Guide hostess badge. Headed 'Windsor Castle, 22 March 1944' the Princess wrote:

Dear Lady Godiva,
I am so thrilled with your invitation to your dance which sounds such fun – I shall do my very best to bring a partner and would Lord Tulip do?

Wasn't it wonderful fun at the Meet on Monday? I did think Lady Adcock overdid it a bit with that hat of hers at church – didn't you?

> Thank you again so much,
> yours affectionately,
> Diaphenia

It may appear to be stating the obvious to say that laughter was an ever-present facet of the Royal Family's life, but given the distance between royal parents and children of past generations, the closeness of King George VI, Queen Elizabeth and their daughters was remarkable. Furthermore their contentment in each other's company was always reflected in everything they undertook together. One minor example of this was the King's evident pleasure in the Princesses Elizabeth and Margaret when, in December 1940, they took part in a nativity play. This was the production that had been cancelled at Birkhall the previous year because of the diphtheria scare. Now it was put on at Windsor, so often the setting of the *tableaux vivant*, staged for Queen Victoria's delight by her family.

Local schoolboys were cast as shepherds, Princess Elizabeth – complete with golden crown – played one of the three oriental kings and Princess Margaret took the lead as the Little Child. After the performance, King George, having listened intently to his younger daughter sing 'Gentle Jesus, Meek and Mild', noted in his diary, 'I wept through most of it'.

From this single production was born the wartime pantomimes staged in the Waterloo Chamber. Once again, the Royal Family's almost inherent love of amateur theatricals was given full rein. *Cinderella* was staged in 1941, followed by *The Sleeping Beauty* in 1942. *Aladdin* – in which the Princesses' young cousins, the Duke of Kent and Princess Alexandra were also cast – was produced in 1943 and *Old Mother Red Riding Boots* in 1944. A star role did not always appeal to Princess Margaret, however, and when *The Sleeping Beauty* was cast she firmly stood her ground against taking the lead. Not only did she feel that she had 'hogged' the limelight quite long enough but, as she explains, 'I didn't think I was pretty enough. Another girl in the company was.'

A further outlet for royal talents was the newly formed Madrigal Society. Both Princesses were enthusiastic members of the society, which included some of the young Guards officers and a handful of boys from Eton. Among the latter was the Honourable Angus Ogilvy, who was to marry Princess Alexandra of Kent almost twenty years later.

For the King and Queen, scarcely a day passed during these years when they were not to be found walking the bomb-blasted streets of London or the provinces. Their morale-boosting progresses were ceaseless and wherever they travelled they always chose to meet as many local people as possible. Lord Harlech, the Midlands Commissioner, told Harold Nicolson of a visit the royal couple made to Sheffield one winter. As their car stopped, he said, 'The Queen nips out into the snow and goes straight into the middle of the crowd and starts talking to them. First they would just gape; then they all started talking at once – 'Hi! Your Majesty! Look here!''.'

Never were the King and Queen oblivious to the hardships their subjects endured. They climbed over rubble inspecting bomb damage, they offered help in whatever way they could (on one occasion the Queen successfully managed to coax a small but terrified dog out of a hole where it lay cringing); they shared air-raid shelters with ordinary folk, offered words of comfort and sympathy to the bereaved, and commiserated with those made homeless. Nobody doubted their sincerity or their anguish at what they saw; nor indeed was their presence ever considered an empty parade of *noblesse oblige*. There were no meaningless gestures and no well-rehearsed platitudes.

Although it was not widely known at the time, the King and Queen had themselves experienced an alarming brush with death. It occurred on 12 September 1940 when a German bomber, taking full advantage of low cloud cover, flew straight up the Mall to deposit two sticks of six bombs each on Buckingham Palace. The King and Queen had been working together in their room when 'all of a sudden we heard an aircraft making a zooming noise above us,' wrote the King, 'saw 2 bombs falling past the opposite side of the Palace, & then heard 2 resounding crashes as the bombs fell in the quadrangle about 30 yards away. We looked at each other & then we were out in the passage as fast as we could get there ... We all wondered why we weren't dead. ...'

Had it not been for the memorial to Queen Victoria which has stood on its great stone island in front of the palace since 1911, they might well have been killed. Nonetheless the damage to Buckingham Palace was extensive. The private chapel was no more, smashed railings lay among the debris of the forecourt, twisted window frames gaped black and empty and, from the broken sewers, rats invaded the building.

Throughout the war the Princesses' public appearances were naturally infrequent, but in 1943, after the Anglo-American offensive had reaped great success against Rommel's forces in North Africa, Princess Margaret and her sister went to London. The occasion was the celebratory Te Deum held in St Paul's Cathedral on 19 May. Accompanying the King and Queen, the Princesses were, as Chips Channon noted in his diary, 'dressed alike in blue, which made them seem like little girls'; but little girls they were not. On the contrary, 'all the notabilities of England' gathered in the cathedral were aware that the two girls were poised on the verge of womanhood. Princess Elizabeth had celebrated her seventeenth birthday in April and, in August, Princess Margaret would enter her fourteenth year.

From about this time, the British press, so besotted by the Princesses as children, began to follow their progress with a new intensity as their individual personalities began to emerge more clearly. Princess Elizabeth, now almost an adult, attracted rather more attention than her younger sister, which gave rise to stories of jealousy between them. Such stories were more speculative than factual, but as was to be seen in the years ahead apocryphal stories knew wide currency and tall stories always seem to grow taller in the retelling. Even the King himself is supposed to have remarked that the time had come to keep a notebook entitled 'Things My Daughters Never Did' and another on the subject of things his daughters never said.

Be that as it may, Princess Elizabeth, as her father's heir, was inevitably involved in areas that were denied her sister. The sovereign's famous red boxes containing state papers was one immediate example. Another was the tuition in constitutional history that Princess Elizabeth received from Sir Henry Marten, Vice-Provost of Eton. But on neither count did Princess Margaret feel deprived. Her sister's *official* seniority and all that this involved, together with an understanding that other members of the Royal Family are never made privy to issues of concern to the sovereign and his heir, were matters that she accepted as a fact of life.

One such issue – at least according to the news media – was an imminent change of title for Princess Elizabeth. To mark her eighteenth birthday, the press claimed that she was about to be created Princess of Wales in her own right. In fact speculation to this effect became so intense that the King, with the concurrence of Winston Churchill and the War Cabinet, was forced to issue a firm denial.

'How could I create Lilibet the Princess of Wales', His Majesty wrote to Queen Mary, 'when it is the recognised title of the wife of the Prince of Wales? Her own name is so nice and what name would she be called by when she marries I want to know?'

Princess of Wales or not, 1944 saw an important step in Princess Elizabeth's career, one which provided another target for Princess Margaret's alleged envy. This was when the King finally agreed to allow his elder daughter to 'join-up'. Her consistent choice had been the A.T.S. (Auxiliary Territorial Service). No 230873 Second Subaltern The Princess Elizabeth learned how to strip and service an engine, and became proficient in vehicle maintenance, although she was never to see 'action' beyond her training centre which, according to the omnipresent censor, was located 'somewhere in England'. All the same the Princess proudly found herself in uniform which, according to the royal governess, Miss Crawford, made Princess Margaret 'very cross'.

What seems to emerge from Miss Crawford's memoirs is an apparent bias in favour of Princess Elizabeth, which ultimately produced a distorted image of the young Princess Margaret. It is not suggested that the governess was in any way guilty of malice by publicly reminiscing about her years in royal service; she may simply have seen it as a way to ensure an income after her retirement, soon to come into effect. But by her lack of forethought, Miss Crawford – or Mrs George Buthlay as she became in 1947 – betrayed her employer's trust. Moreover, her inevitable fall from grace was precipitated by the way she handled the matter, for it was only after an American publishing house had accepted the manuscript of her book, *The Little Princesses*, that Crawfie approached the Queen. Sympathetic though Her Majesty was, the desired royal assent was not forthcoming. The Queen realized that such a book could only constitute an invasion of her family's privacy. The governess was therefore asked to curb her literary ambitions.

Yet, even at this stage she decided not to confess that, despite her request, she had, in fact, presented the Queen with a *fait accompli*. Unwittingly the American publishers dealt the final hand in this unusual game when proofs were sent to Nancy, Lady Astor, who in turn submitted them to the Queen. The story does not end there, however, for Miss Crawford went on to write several more stories about her former charges and in her retirement sent frequent letters of request to the Queen. Among her less astonishing requests was that she be appointed a lady-in-waiting to one of the Princesses.

It was the first book, though, not the later stories, that did the damage: from it Princess Elizabeth emerged whiter than white, an irreproachably angelic young woman, while Princess Margaret, on the other hand, was made to appear wilful, spoilt and ultimately resentful of the office her sister would one day inherit. Though it is true to say that Princess Margaret always resented being cast as 'the younger sister', there is no evidence to support the belief that she would have been happier had the roles been reversed. In fact, Princess Margaret is adamant that she has never coveted her sister's crown.

In writing *The Little Princesses*, which was first published in Britain in 1950, Crawfie made insufficient allowance for the normal childhood behaviour of her charges. By emphasizing their differences, their small rivalries and upsets, she misrepresented the bond of love and understanding that has always existed betweeen them. She also placed undue emphasis on the suggestions made by Queen Mary in regard to her granddaughters' education, largely neglecting the interest shown by the Princesses' parents in their development.

Princess Margaret's formal induction into the sphere of public service did not, of course, take place until after the war had ended; but she was given the opportunity to experience a little of things to come in July 1944, for it was then, at the age of thirteen, that she paid an official visit to the school that bears her name in Windsor. On this occasion, wearing a pink cotton dress and wide-brimmed straw hat, the Princess, under the watchful eye of her mother, made her first public speech, feeling 'dreadfully sick' with nerves. Ever since the Princess has always disliked public speaking.

Nearly a year later, on 5 May 1945, victory in Europe was celebrated with all the fervour it is possible to imagine. Patriotism ran high and to demonstrate it cheering people, in their tens of thousands, flocked to Buckingham Palace. As the King and Queen with the Princesses and Winston Churchill stepped on to the palace balcony, there was no doubt in anybody's mind about the love and unity binding each and every person there.

'We went out eight times altogether during the afternoon and evening,' noted the King in his diary. 'We were given a great reception.'

That evening the Princesses themselves joined the throng outside Buckingham Palace. Accompanied by a group of officers, they slipped unobtrusively through the palace gates to join in the fun. A policeman's helmet was playfully knocked off by their uncle, David Bowes-Lyon, who offered a tongue-in-cheek apology as the Princesses 'ran off, just in case we were caught'.

Later, the group of royal revellers returned along the Mall to join in the vast crowd's noisy demands for the King and Queen. Having waited for a short time, the Princesses sent a message in to the palace saying they were outside and would their Majesties oblige just once more? When the doors of the balcony were opened yet again the Princesses were caught up in the cheering.

Six weeks later Japan surrendered and VJ-Day – 15 August – brought scenes of renewed celebration. The following week Princess Margaret celebrated her fifteenth birthday and, on 25 August, the Royal Family travelled north to Balmoral for its first, albeit brief, peacetime holiday.

The nation started the process of adjustment to life without hostilities and slowly began to repair the war damage and restore some of the old ways of life. The Royal Opera House, Covent Garden, which had suffered the indignity of being used as a dance-hall during the war years, was officially reopened on 20 February 1946 with a gala performance of the ballet *The Sleeping Beauty*. The Royal Family attended and watched spell-bound as Margot Fonteyn danced the role of Aurora against sets designed by Oliver Messel who, little more than a decade later, was to become Princess Margaret's uncle-in-law.

The following month, on 26 March, Princess Margaret undertook her first solo official engagement. She had been invited by the Save The Children Fund (of which her niece Princess Anne is today President) to open a new play centre in Camden, North London. Known then as the Hopscotch Inn, it provided facilities for local children ranging in age from three years to sixteen to take part in a variety of pastimes, including handicrafts, games, drama and dancing. One of the youngest members at that time was Fella Strozek, the daughter of a Polish seaman. It was she who was selected to present the customary bouquet to the royal visitor with the greeting 'Princess Margaret, we welcome you to our club and do hope you will enjoy your visit.'

Today she recalls that, because of its close proximity to Euston railway station, which was a prime target for the bombs of the Luftwaffe, Camden had been severely damaged. 'I think that is why the Hopscotch Inn had been built ... to keep us children off the bomb sites, which were still very dangerous.' Recalling the Princess's visit, she says, 'I remember her very clearly. She was so natural and charming, but at the same time one could tell that she was royal. After I had given her the bouquet and made my speech, she took my hand and asked me to show her all the classes. I remember she wanted to see everything at the centre.'

Also present at the Hopscotch Inn that day was the broadcaster Audrey Russell. Recently returned from Europe where she was the B.B.C.'s only fully accredited female war correspondent, Miss Russell was despatched to Camden to report on Princess Margaret's official debut. 'One has to remember that she was only fifteen,' she recalls, 'but I was first struck by her marvellous poise. I think she was trying very hard to follow her mother's example, talking to everybody and asking questions all the time. . . .'

CHAPTER FIVE

A ROYAL AMBASSADOR

At sixteen, rising seventeen, Princess Margaret was still in the class-room, by now Crawfie's only pupil, and eager to complete her studies. To the Princess's rescue came the Vicomtesse de Bellaigue, with whom she made visits to art galleries and to exhibitions of some of the nation's greatest treasures, like the Wallace Collection, which had been stored outside London for the duration of the war. Today Princess Margaret acknowledges the Vicomtesse – whose son Geoffrey is Surveyor of The Queen's Works of Art – as one of the greatest cultural influences in her life.

The return of pictures and objects in the Royal Collection to Buckingham Palace and Windsor Castle helped stimulate the Princess's interest further at an impressionable moment in her life. Her taste in art is broad, but today her personal acquisitions are largely works by twentieth-century artists such as Jean Cocteau, John Piper, Edward Seago and Brian Organ. In addition to official visits to galleries, Princess Margaret will occasionally take a party of friends for a private evening view of an exhibition at the Queen's Gallery.

Although Princess Margaret awaited the end of her schooldays in much the same spirit as most teenagers who are keen to experience life for themselves, there were still subjects to be studied and revised. As 1946 drew to a close and the new year opened, two such subjects were the history and geography of South Africa, plus tuition in Afrikaans. The incentive for these studies was the Royal Family's imminent departure for that country. The idea of a royal tour had first been planted in the King's mind by South Africa's Prime

Minister, Field Marshal Jan Smuts, during his wartime visits to London.

Once a staunch republican and a former supreme commander of Queen Victoria's enemy army during the Boer War, Smuts was by this time a vigorous royalist with absolute belief in the power of monarchy. Kings and queens, he said, were capable of influencing public opinion and, with a general election due in South Africa in 1948, the advantages of a royal tour at this juncture spoke clearly for themselves.

At home both the King and his Government were of one mind: the visit would strengthen the bonds of empire. Moreover, it was hoped that, although extensive, the tour might prove beneficial to the King himself. It would stimulate his mind (as had his earlier visits to Canada, Australia and New Zealand) and help restore the vitality sapped by the physical strain of war. For Princess Margaret and her sister, their first overseas tour would provide an important foretaste of what was to become a major feature of their official lives.

Among the South Africans – whom, the Royal Family had been warned, were not a demonstrative people – the arrival of the royal novitiates was awaited with as much curiosity as that of their parents, who were past masters in the diplomatic art of public relations. The warning words proved needless, for wherever the royal party travelled on its 23,000-mile progress – through cities, towns, even isolated railroad stations in the open spaces of the veld – crowds gathered to watch and applaud. The King and Queen disappointed nobody; their stamina throughout the twelve-week schedule seemed inexhaustible.

Of their daughters, Princess Margaret was proclaimed to be the livelier by members of the South African press. To them Princess Elizabeth appeared shy, even grave, while Princess Margaret's vivacity and her – as yet embryonic – 'presence' were widely remarked upon.

The Royal Family, or 'we four' as the King sometimes liked to put it, returned to England at the end of April. The King had lost a stone in weight, but despite this he looked fit and well; and while health problems were soon to give rise to family concern, he at least felt that this tour had done him 'a great deal of good'.

In July 1947 Princess Elizabeth's engagement was finally announced, following months of speculation, and on 20 November she and the newly created Duke of Edinburgh were married at Westminster Abbey. Winston Churchill saw the royal wedding as, 'A flash of colour on the hard road we have to travel'. But to Princess Margaret, who had acted as chief bridesmaid, gaining a brother-in-law was poor compensation for what she keenly felt was the loss of her closest companion. She became, as might have beeen expected, a regular visitor at Clarence House, St James's Palace, where her sister went to live, but it was only too plain that Princess Elizabeth's life had assumed a separate and even more distinct direction.

There is an often told story that, until Princess Elizabeth married, she and her sister had been code-named 'P[rincess] 1' and 'P[rincess] 2' by staff at Buckingham Palace. Today Princess Margaret refutes the truth of this story: 'I was never known as P2.' But no matter what the truth, she was now the *only* Princess in residence at the palace, and by the end of 1947 she had emerged from what may be considered a protracted adolescence to a position of growing importance. This was to be seen more particularly during 1948, for in that year, her public life began to operate on a full-time basis.

Of this period in her life, various allegations were to be made in later years; one such by Nigel Dempster was that King George VI had 'resisted any inclination to encourage [Princess Margaret] to find a purpose in life'. In response it can only be said that the purpose of Princess Margaret's life was no different to that of any other member of the Royal Family: to fulfil the obligations of her role as a representative of the Crown.

An equally unrealistic claim is that Queen Elizabeth faltered in her encouragement of her younger daughter because she 'felt sure that Margaret was but a year or two away from marriage to an eminently suitable aristocrat' and would 'only occasionally [be] called upon to perform royal duties'.

Firstly, only Princess Margaret's marriage to an aristocrat based permanently abroad, perhaps somebody of foreign birth, would have precluded her continued participation in the royal round. Secondly, until the latter half of the 1950s, the Royal Family comprised too few members able to play an active part in public duties for Princess Margaret not to have a full role. Of the King's surviving brothers, the Duke of Windsor lived in exile and the Duke of Gloucester, like the Princess Royal, their only sister, already maintained separate programmes of official commitments. This left Princess Elizabeth (though her schedules were curtailed by pregnancies in 1948 and 1950), the Duke of Edinburgh, Princess Margaret and the Duchess of Kent (Princess Marina) to shoulder the great plethora of royal duties between them. Edward, Alexandra and Michael of Kent, like their cousins William and Richard of Gloucester, had yet to graduate from the schoolroom and the question of official roles for the Earl of Harewood and the Hon. Gerald Lascelles, sons of the Princess Royal, never arose.

The most important of all Princess Margaret's duties during 1948 took her on a four-day visit to the Netherlands from 6 to 9 September. Two weeks before her departure the Princess had celebrated her eighteenth birthday and now, for the first time, she was to act as the King's personal representative at the Installation of the new Dutch sovereign, Queen Juliana. After the new Queen herself, Princess Margaret was the most popular figure among her host nation and, despite the large number of senior European royalties in Amsterdam, it was she – though very much to her embarrassment – who was specifically invited to inspect the guard of honour drawn up outside the royal palace.

In his biography of Princess Alice, Countess of Athlone, who was also present at the Installation, Theo Aronson has written: 'Almost overnight, it seemed, [Princess Margaret] in her floor-length pink dress and pink ostrich feather hat had developed into a stylish and beautiful Princess: "too sweet, charming and shy, and lovely to look upon", as Princess Alice puts it.'

In Princess Margaret's inaugural or coming-out year – 'such as it was after the war' she says – more than fifty public engagements had been arranged to help ease her into her job. As Colonel-in-Chief she attended the presentation of the Freedom of the City of Glasgow to the Highland Light Infantry; she visited the Bath Assembly; launched the merchant vessel *British Mariner*; attended the Brunswick Ball for Boys Clubs in Edinburgh; toured Scotland with her parents, returning via York; visited Barnardo Homes in Tunbridge Wells; attended a gala performance of *Coppelia* in aid of Denville Hall for Old Actors and Actresses, and visited Glyndebourne Festival for Sir Thomas Beecham's lecture and the first part of the orchestral concert.

Later in the year Princess Margaret, attended by Miss Jennifer Bevan, her newly appointed first lady-in-waiting, visited the London

Missionary Society for the naming of a new ship, the *John Williams* VI; she attended a reception for the Commonwealth Parliamentary Association; was present at the opening of the Ceylon Government offices in London; took part in the State Visit of the Shah of Persia; attended the Harvest Thanksgiving Service at Westminster Abbey, the Royal Command (Variety) Performance and the Royal Film Performance, and was present at the Royal Albert Hall for the British Legion Festival of Remembrance and at the Home Office in Whitehall, from where she witnessed the Act of Remembrance at the Cenotaph on Armistice Day.

While 1948 was a significant year in Princess Margaret's life, there were also special events in the lives of other members of her family. The Silver Wedding of the King and Queen on 26 April was marked by public and private festivities, and seven months later, on 14 November, Princess Elizabeth presented her parents with their first grandchild. News of Prince Charles's birth reached Princess Margaret during an official visit to Sheffield for a pageant of youth entitled *The Pageant of Production*, and in delight she privately joked that from now on she would doubtless be known as 'Charlie's Aunt'.

In all the Royal Family's happiness, however, an anxious note was struck when it became increasingly apparent that all was far from well with the King. From the beginning of the year, though he had said nothing, he had been suffering from cramp in both legs. In the months that followed, his condition had grown steadily worse until, by October, his left foot was continuously numb and at night intense pain prevented him from sleeping. By the end of November the King's right foot had been similarly affected.

His Majesty's doctors were consulted and they diagnosed arteriosclerosis. By now, with the threat of gangrene, fears grew that his right leg might have to be amputated. In the event such drastic action was averted, though surgery was not. So it was that four months later, in March 1949, the sovereign underwent a right lumbar sympathectomy operation with satisfactory results. Nonetheless the spring tour of Australia and New Zealand that George VI was to have undertaken with the Queen and Princess Margaret had to be postponed, much to the King's distress. 'It would be hazardous for His Majesty to embark upon a long journey,' said a statement issued by the royal physicians.

By June King George had recovered sufficiently to attend the annual Birthday Parade (Trooping the Colour), though not on horseback as is the tradition. The idea that her father should participate in the parade riding in an open landau was put forward by Princess Margaret. In a *landau*, His Majesty responded? It had never been heard of – the sovereign always rode his own horse! The Princess remonstrated that a carriage was drawn by horses and in the end her persistence paid off. By November the King's recovery was such that his doctors' optimism led to talk of reviving plans for the royal tour of the Antipodes.

Foreign travel for Princess Margaret, in her own right, was also in the air at the start of 1949, when Major Tom Harvey, Private Secretary to Queen Elizabeth, suggested that the Princess might make a tour of Italy to see the battlefields. Both the King and Queen agreed to the idea without reservation, and so that April Princess Margaret left London at the start of a five-week European trip. With her travelled Major Harvey and his wife Lady Mary, together with two others, one of whom was Her Royal Highness's personal detective.

The first stop on the Princess's itinerary, which reads like an advertisement for a de-luxe package trip, was Naples, where she was greeted by the British Ambassador and his wife, Sir Victor Mallet and Lady Mallet, as well as by the Prefect and Mayor of the City. To the excited Italians Princess Margaret became *la bella Margherita*, and they dogged her steps in droves, so much so that any hope that this might remain a private visit was dashed almost from the start. Some days later, as the crowds that surrounded her every move seemed unwilling to keep their distance, the *Giornale d'Italia* complained in an editorial that such excessive interest in the Princess's visit was preventing her from enjoying the sights. Instead, it said, all she had was a fine view of the backs of the *carabinieri*, as they wrestled to clear a path for her. It seems hardly likely that the editorial had much influence, but matters did begin to improve. All the same, the interest of the Italian press continued unabated and one newspaper successfully bribed a chambermaid to allow reporters into the Princess's hotel bedroom. The result was the release of details about everything they had seen, right down to the make and colour of her nail varnish.

From Naples, the royal party moved on to Capri, Sorrento, Pompeii and Salerno where the Princess laid roses on the grave of one British soldier. It was a random but well-publicized choice and the Princess was moved to find a letter of thanks from the soldier's mother when she returned to London.

In Rome Princess Margaret was to have an audience with Pope Pius XII, an appointment she kept despite her trepidation. 'I was so nervous that I couldn't stop shaking,' the Princess remembers. On her arrival at the Vatican, dressed in a long black coat and lace mantilla, she was received by Cardinal Mantini (Archbishop of Milan and later Pope Paul VI), whom she found to be 'a great comfort', assuring her how much His Holiness was looking forward to their meeting. The audience turned out to be a great success and, at the end of it, the Pontiff shyly asked if he might give the Princess a gift. It was a small crucifix which Princess Margaret was pleased to accept, to the obvious relief of the Pope who, it appears, was not at all sure it was the right gift to offer to a devout Protestant Princess. (Princess Margaret's religious conviction was such that she had sought permission to be confirmed at the age of fourteen. In the event she was told she must wait two years until she was sixteen, the age at which Princess Elizabeth had also been confirmed.)

After Rome and Siena came Florence – the city she found the most fascinating of the entire tour – Bologna, Venice and Stresa before the Princess and her party crossed the Simplon Pass. In Switzerland they were the guests of ex-Queen Victoria-Eugenie of Spain, Princess Margaret's 'Cousin Ena', who in her retirement had chosen to live in Lausanne. At the end of the visit, the former Queen remarked that her young cousin had 'blossomed out deliciously', adding with some satisfaction, 'What a success she will be in Paris', the Princess's next and final destination.

There can be no doubt that Princess Margaret was indeed a success in Paris, but she found the press there even more tiresome than in Italy. Every man she danced with when she attended a charity ball was being lined up as a prospective bridegroom, and reporters and photographers were to be found hot on her heels when she visited the salon of Christian Dior to 'have a look' at some of his new creations.

After the magnificence of Italy and the elegance of Paris, Princess Margaret plunged into her second year of official engagements: visits to the offices of the *Daily Graphic*, to the English Speaking Union, the St John's Ambulance Cadets in Eastbourne, the Wandsworth Youth Week, the Edinburgh Festival, et cetera.

Among her official engagements she made private visits of an educational nature. For example, with Princess Elizabeth, whom she persuaded to join her (later, as sovereign, she would never have the opportunity of witnessing the execution of justice in her name), Princess Margaret visited the Old Bailey and sat through a trial for attempted murder. She visited Scotland Yard, the Juvenile Courts and a Citizens' Advice Bureau; toured Battersea Power Station, the Thomas Coram School and saw how mass radiography worked in the detection of tuberculosis. 'All these', as Princess Margaret explains, 'were to help give me a broader understanding of life in general.'

At this time, however, the press began to look away from the majority of her public functions to focus attention on the social aspects of her life, even if there was nothing particularly outstanding about her choice of companions. Indeed, since Princess Margaret was still bound by the inflexible social conventions of the time and had yet to become more adventurous in overcoming society's prejudices, those around her were predictably from society's uppermost reaches.

Then in 1949 the Princess met the gregarious Sharman Douglas, daughter of the American Ambassador to the Court of St James's. Through the friendship which developed between them Princess Margaret met a number of lively young people who frequently gathered at the United States Embassy, one of the few places in London where they could enjoy themselves away from prying eyes. Of course the media tenaciously exploited the Princess's friendship with Sharman Douglas and her circle, and overnight, or so it now seems, created the 'Margaret Set'.

'Most of the people who became my friends – and they generally had other and much closer friends of their own – were Sharman's friends first,' Princess Margaret says today. 'So if anything, it was *her* set, not mine. There never was a "Margaret Set".'

Nonetheless, Princess Margaret, Sharman Douglas and their friends invariably made news in those dismal, austere days in post-war Britain. Before long each of the men who belonged to Princess Margaret's 'inner circle' was being closely scrutinized, lest one should be seen to surpass another in her affections. A romance, in the eyes of the press, would have added extra excitement to this glamorous group's sorties to restaurants, parties and night-clubs.

It was not long before the public became familiar with the names of the men in Princess Margaret's life – the founder members of her circle were Johnny Dalkeith, Sunny Blandford, Billy Wallace, Simon Phipps and Dominic Elliot. Most of the men she knew had served in the forces, the Guards or the Royal Navy, before branching out into business. Some, like the Earl of Dalkeith and the Marquess of Blandford, knew that they would have to change direction again – into the management of their estates – once they succeeded their fathers as Dukes of Buccleuch and Marlborough respectively. Simon Phipps entered the Church, while Billy Wallace made valiant attempts to become established as a businessman, though constant ill health prevented this. Of the Princess's women friends, however, rather less has ever been known; indeed, most of those she considers her closest friends remain to this day unfamiliar figures to the public and the news media, a fact the Princess is proud to point out.

'Girls of one's own age were not really interested in what one did officially,' the Princess has said, 'but one's men friends were polite enough to listen.' Foremost among the handful of women of whom Princess Margaret was especially fond was Lady Caroline Montagu-Douglas-Scott, a niece of the Duchess of Gloucester and the sister of Johnny Dalkeith. 'A very best friend', it was she who had effectively bridged the gap in the Princess's life after Princess Elizabeth married. Then, of course, came Sharman Douglas and later still – during the early 1950s – the equally gregarious Judy Montagu, who was already a great friend of Billy Wallace.

Indicative of the kind of press stories constantly to be read about Princess Margaret at this time was her attendance at a dinner party given by Sharman Douglas. It followed an official engagement the Princess had undertaken in London's East End, but while the official part of her evening was ignored by the press, the unofficial part was not. The following morning, gossip columns told how Princess Margaret had stayed at the party until 4 a.m. dancing the foxtrot, samba and charleston with the Lords Ogilvy, Blandford and Westmorland. On another occasion, the Princess, accompanied by Sunny Blandford among others, attended a Halloween Ball at the Dorchester Hotel. During the evening, one journalist noted, 'neither the Princess nor her friend, Sharman Douglas, had any success at the hoop-la stall'.

Easy though it is to scoff at the relevance of such items today, it has to be remembered that, both at home and abroad, Princess Margaret had been adopted in a quite remarkable manner. Summing up this phenomenon, one American magazine asserted: 'She is Britain's number one item for public scrutiny. People are more interested in her than in the House of Commons or the dollar crisis.' Indeed, insofar as royalty ever trail-blaze, the Princess was considered to be the trend-setter of her day. When she finally branched out and began experimenting with new hairstyles, for example, countless women followed her lead. As she gradually turned her back on the tried and tested designs of royal dressmakers, copies of her new outfits – though scarcely revolutionary – paid substantial dividends to astute fashion houses. Perhaps she caused the biggest stir by smoking in public. The first time this was noticed was when she was nineteen and dining with friends in a West End restaurant. After dinner she lit up a cigarette in a long ivory holder. It was yet another royal 'fad' to be aped, even though it may have been forgotten that Princess Marina, when she was Duchess of Kent, had done exactly the same thing during the 1930s.

For the opposite sex, photographs of Princess Margaret were at this time as collectable as those of busty Hollywood starlets. This in itself was a novelty, for while patriotic citizens tended to keep likenesses of royalty for reasons of sentiment or loyalty, no princess had ever found herself on a par with British and American sex symbols.

To her official role, however, Princess Margaret brought something more than glamour. Indeed the often quoted 'youthful breeziness' she brought to the corridors of Buckingham Palace led in turn to a gradual relaxation of the rigid attitudes that not only kept royalty out of reach, but out of touch with reality. As one of her friends puts it, 'Materially Princess Margaret doesn't have to worry about everyday things as we do, but she still understands them and she understands other people's problems.' Of her approach to royal duty, another of her friends says, 'I have always seen a great likeness between Queen Victoria and Princess Margaret. For, like her, the Princess has always wanted to do things in her own way. She regards the royal system with the greatest respect, but she has always tried to be more informal about it in her approach to her own duties.'

Inevitably there were those, both inside and outside court circles, on whom the Princess would never make a favourable impression.

Among them was the Canadian Lord Beaverbrook, owner of the London *Daily Express*. To the present day, the reasons for his unmitigated attacks on her remain unclear. It is quite probable, however, that Beaverbrook's use of Princess Margaret as a kind of royal scapegoat stemmed from his long-standing, on-off, love-hate relationship with Lord Mountbatten.

The Beaverbrook-Mountbatten friendship had waxed and waned over many years. Dickie Mountbatten's 'golden boy' aura, his good looks, his charm, his contacts, his semi-royal status, aroused both an admiration and an irrational jealousy in the self-made newspaper baron. Little excuse was required for the suspension of communications between the two men. They had fallen out during the 1920s over a friend of Lady Mountbatten with whom Beaverbrook had struck up an affair and they had clashed again during the mid-1930s over the abdication of Edward VIII.

Yet although Beaverbrook was a great supporter of the Duke of Windsor, he was also said to have admired his successor. If that were true, it is difficult to appreciate why he should have been so keen to malign George VI's younger daughter. Princess Margaret has said, 'I was always told that it was because Lord Beaverbrook couldn't openly attack my father; my sister never did anything wrong – and anyway, she married the right man – so he attacked me instead.'

With or without good reason, the *Express* campaign against the Princess continued in full flood into the mid-1970s. By then, of course, Beaverbrook was dead and his son, Max Aitken (or 'Little Max' as he is known), had assumed command. At about this time Aitken came face to face with Princess Margaret over lunch one day and immediately decided to call a halt to the newspaper's 'witch-hunt'.

'That girl's got the most beautiful eyes!' he exclaimed. 'I think it's about time we stopped knocking her.'

Aitken's heart may have been softened by the beauty of Princess Margaret's eyes – 'the only thing about me worth looking at' she says – but to the rest of Fleet Street, they were, at best, a minor consideration. Her name made good copy, it helped to sell newspapers; it was 'business as usual'.

Attempts by the media to satisfy the demand for news of Princess Margaret meant that fact and fiction soon became, and remained, inseparable. To attempt an accurate character analysis of Princess

Margaret today means disregarding the legend that has been built up, layer by solid layer, over the past thirty years and more. In that time, the views of the press have coloured and influenced public opinion too often and too radically for a fair picture to emerge.

Princess Margaret's character contains many contradictions, if not extremes. Hers is a particularly complex and sometimes exasperatingly decisive personality, but one which soon either wins the affection or incurs the dislike of those who come into contact with her. It is probably true to say that there are no intermediate stages in people's reactions towards her.

In an artistic sense, Princess Margaret is temperamental, rather than volatile as some have claimed. She holds strong, well-reasoned views and has firm, even stubborn, beliefs, which at times make her demanding. Similarly, she has an ability to intimidate, often to an alarming degree. This may be caused by a marked distance in her manner or by her decisive reaction to a given situation, but more especially it arises from what friends call her 'acid-drop look': at times – when she feels threatened or offended – her eyes, which are perhaps best described as cornflower blue, become icy. This characteristic of fixing somebody with a freezing stare is neither the result of an instant change of mood nor a royal demonstration of how to pull rank; it is, as Princess Margaret herself explains, 'a defence mechanism. I'm not aware that I am doing it.'

Against such considerations must be weighed her virtues and it is here that we begin to find the measure of the true Princess Margaret: a woman who, in complete contrast to her reputation, is surprisingly approachable. She is considerate, talented but self-effacing, conventionally inclined (despite the 'jet-setter' label attached to her in the mid-1960s), and, moreover, disarmingly warm. She is, as those who know her well have pointed out, a loyal and dependable friend who, once her trust has been earned, is a friend for life.

'She is incredibly kind and gives so much of herself ... always thinking up treats for others,' said a writer who has enjoyed the Princess's friendship for more than twenty years.

An American journalist once described the Princess as 'gutsy', and in many ways she is. But the accompanying image of her as a querulous, perverse woman who only occasionally reveals some of her nicer traits is considerably wide of the mark. Her ability to intimidate, for example, is indicative of her vulnerability, and her extreme generosity may to some extent reflect her need to feel wanted and of use.

From their earliest years Princess Margaret and her sister, although they underwent no rigidly formal training, were raised to believe that royal duty was inviolable. In some ways they may be seen as the products of a carefully preserved mould which, for generations, has produced responsible, well-disciplined princes and princesses. Princess Margaret's detractors would doubtless disagree. Indeed they claim that she would prefer to keep her position, her state income and her privileges without 'earning' any of them. Those who are better informed can and do make claims to the contrary.

Commander W.R. Miller, Clerk to the Worshipful Company of Haberdashers, wrote to *The Times* in April 1978:

> ... ever since her admission as [a Freeman of the Company], she has paid consistent and meticulous attention to the Company's charitable activities and her conscientiousness in this respect has been a constant source of encouragement to everybody concerned with them.
>
> The Princess has never refused a request from this Company for her active participation in its charitable affairs and my Court of Wardens is deeply indebted to her for her unstinted support.

In her public function, says one of the present Queen's retired advisers, 'Princess Margaret is capable of sheer brilliance.' And the Chief Guide, Lady Baden Powell, has said, 'She really does understand the [Girl Guide] movement inside out ... finances, policy, planning ... and she would always query anything she didn't grasp. She's not in the slightest bit inhibited.'

Ultimately, duty has demanded of Princess Margaret rather more than privilege has restored.

CHAPTER SIX

THE END OF AN ERA

Until the beginning of 1952 the routine of Princess Margaret's life continued much as in the previous few years. Official and unofficial engagements – mostly discussed with her parents beforehand – charted the course of her days, though some of her friends like Sunny Blandford and Johnny Dalkeith were soon ducking the lime-light in favour of marriage.

The American Embassy still saw a great deal of Princess Margaret and from time to time it also welcomed other members of her family. It was there, for example, that the heiress presumptive was found dressed as a maid one evening with her husband dressed as a waiter. Together with an equerry, Princess Elizabeth and the Duke of Edinburgh had attended the Ambassador's fancy-dress ball in the guise of 'The Waiter, the Porter and the Upstairs Maid'. For her part, Princess Margaret linked arms with seven other girls to provide the evening's cabaret. To the music of Offenbach and wearing frilly skirts and high-heeled shoes, they kicked their way through a de-corous version of the *cancan* under the direction of Danny Kaye, the American comedian, who was currently starring in his own show at the London Palladium.

Such occasions provided light relief from the more pressing ques-tion of the King's health, which had again started to deteriorate. In May 1951 he wrote to his mother of 'a condition on the left lung known as pneumonitis ... I was x-rayed and the photographs showed a shadow.' He wrote optimistically, though with some irritation at 'not being able to chuck out the bug'.

His doctors prescribed two months' rest to restore his strength and the sovereign obediently complied. Part of June was spent at Royal Lodge, Windsor, and the rest of the time at his beloved Sandringham. Then, at the beginning of August, 'getting stronger every day', the King took his wife and younger daughter to Balmoral. There, a little under three weeks later, in the company of her parents and some of her friends, Princess Margaret's twenty-first birthday was celebrated. At dinner on 21 August, she cut her birthday cake: brought from London by train, it stood eighteen inches high and was iced in the pattern of her personal coat-of-arms. Afterwards the Princess took part in an eightsome reel, danced on the drive outside the front door to the accompaniment of bagpipes, before her friends and the equerries-in-waiting, all of whom had been issued with torches, organized themselves into a long line, stretching about a hundred yards to a nearby hill. One torch was lit, then another and another, all along the chain. Finally, when the last was alight, its bearer turned to ignite a bonfire that had been specially built in honour of the occasion.

Two months later, as the King lay resting after a further operation for the removal of his left lung, which had proved to be cancerous, Princess Margaret was appointed a Counsellor of State for the first and last time during her father's reign. By 14 December, his fifty-sixth birthday, there seemed good reason to hope that the King was now on the road to recovery. 'An operation is not an illness,' he said reassuringly as he looked forward to Christmas at Sandringham and the promise of some good shooting on the royal estate.

Five weeks later, on 31 January 1952, His Majesty with the Queen and Princess Margaret travelled from Norfolk to take leave of Princess Elizabeth and Prince Philip as they set off from Heathrow Airport on a tour that was to take them to East Africa, Australia and New Zealand. It was a poignant farewell.

On 5 February, a cold but sunny day, Princess Margaret and her mother motored over from Sandringham to Ludham to visit the painter Edward Seago. The King, meanwhile, went out hare-shooting in the very highest of spirits. He returned contented, and spent a relaxing evening in the company of his wife and daughter and a handful of friends. Before going to his room, the King listened to a news broadcast which featured Princess Elizabeth's arrival in Kenya, and then, laughing heartily at a joke he had just heard, retired at 10.30. Shortly afterwards, at about midnight, a watchman noticed him fastening the latch of his bedroom window. Sometime during the small hours of that morning King George VI died.

With the death of the father she adored, Princess Margaret found herself in great need of comfort, both spiritual and temporal. The former was found in the strength of her religious beliefs, her regular attendance at church and the contact she had with her old friend Simon Phipps, at that time a curate in Huddersfield and today the Bishop of Lincoln. The Princess had always been quietly devout, and her simple religious faith has played an important part in her life. After her father's death, she attended post-confirmation classes at St Paul's Vicarage in Knightsbridge and a series of eleven half-hour Lenten lectures on the subject of God and eternal life given by the Bishop of Kensington. The Archbishop of Canterbury later said of her, 'I knew what a genuine concern she had in the life of the Church and the life of a churchwoman.'

For temporal comfort, however, she turned increasingly to the equerry of whom her father had been particularly fond. Group Captain Peter Townsend had been appointed to the King's staff eight years earlier, when a new policy was introduced of honouring officers who had distinguished themselves during the war. Prior to this, all the sovereign's equerries had been chosen on a personal basis. This new system catered for temporary appointments, originally intended to last for three months.

'If you don't find the idea particularly revolting,' Air Chief Marshal Sir Charles Portal, Chief of the Air Staff, told Townsend, 'I propose recommending you....' Waiting outside the Air Ministry building in Whitehall that day as her husband learned of his new posting was Rosemary Townsend who, when told of Portal's proposal, exclaimed with delight, 'We're made.'

'It was natural ... for her to be glad,' Townsend wrote in his autobiography thirty years later, 'but how tragically mistaken she was. For from now on we were destined, as a married couple, to be "un-made".' The 'un-making' of the Townsend marriage effectively began in March 1944, when the Group Captain arrived at Buckingham Palace to take up his duties.

On 20 December 1952, ten months after the King's death, a brief notice in the press advised: 'Group Captain Peter Wooldridge

Townsend … was granted a decree nisi in the Divorce Court yesterday on the grounds of misconduct by his wife Cecil Rosemary. Mr John de Laszlo, an export merchant, was cited as co-respondent. . . .'

The events which led to the Townsend divorce are not directly relevant to the story of Princess Margaret, but clearly his prolonged absences during the eight years he had served as equerry imposed a strain that neither Peter nor Rosemary had forseen.

By the middle of 1952 the Group Captain had assumed greater responsibility in the line of royal duty, for he had, at the request of Queen Elizabeth the Queen Mother (as the King's widow chose to be styled) accepted the office of Comptroller to her Household. By this time the Queen Mother and Princess Margaret had moved out of Buckingham Palace into Clarence House and, in the inevitable reshuffling of staff and apartments, Clarence House also became to all intents and purposes Townsend's permanent base.

Princess Margaret was aware of her love for Peter Townsend long before it was reciprocated. It was not, in fact, until the summer of 1952 that the Group Captain was able to put a name to his feelings and, even then, he did not declare it until the spring of 1953. He chose to do so while the Royal Family was staying at Windsor Castle where, says the Princess, she and Townsend had first met.

The next step in what the contemporary press called 'one of the greatest romances of history' was for the Princess to tell her sister and her mother that she and Townsend would like to marry. 'If disconcerted, as they had every reason to be,' Townsend wrote later, 'they did not flinch, but faced it with perfect calm and, it must be said, considerable charity.'

Privately the new Queen was delighted that Princess Margaret had found such happiness, but the difficulties posed by Townsend's divorce influenced her official reaction as sovereign. The Queen Mother, however, still battling with her grief at the King's sudden demise, closed her eyes to the situation and chose to ignore its existence.

During a talk with her sister and the Group Captain, the Queen, who had asked to see them both together, made it clear that she could give no personal directive. It was a matter the couple had to resolve for themselves, notwithstanding the opposition they would come up against. But Her Majesty did have one request: 'Under the circumstances', she said, 'it isn't unreasonable for me to ask you to wait a year.'

The Queen's request may well have rested on the possibility that, within twelve months, the couple might have changed their minds about marrying. Alternatively, an acceptable solution might have been found. Whichever way one looks at it, the Princess's wish to marry a divorcé placed the Queen, as temporal Governor of the Church of England, in a particularly vulnerable position; as Defender of the Faith she could scarcely overlook canon No 107 of 1603 which expressly forbade divorce.

After the couple had been to see the Queen, Townsend went to discuss the matter with her Private Secretary, Sir Alan ('Tommy') Lascelles. His initial reaction was as unexpected as it was unwelcome. Though Princess Margaret says she knew nothing of it at the time, Lascelles had exclaimed to Townsend, 'You must be either mad or bad.'

'Though not entitled, perhaps, to any sympathy from him, it would all the same have helped,' Townsend wrote later. 'He was a friend and I was asking for his help. I was describing to him a state of affairs which, if thoroughly undesirable, reprehensible even, in his eyes (and, eventually, in a good many others'), was, equally, impossible to ignore.'

Lascelles, however, did not ignore the situation and, though he at no time spoke directly to Princess Margaret on the subject, for he had very little time for her as a person, he did make it clear that her marriage to Townsend was not an impossibility. 'Had he said we *couldn't* get married,' says the Princess today, 'we wouldn't have thought any more about it. But nobody bothered to explain anything to us.'

In the short term, Tommy Lascelles's advice to the Queen was that Townsend should be relieved of his position at Clarence House and found an appointment somewhere abroad. His suggestion was, of course, tantamount to deportation. Yet while the Queen agreed to Townsend's removal from her mother's household, she felt his total banishment was too heartless a move. Instead she appointed him to her own personal staff as an equerry.

In the meantime, Lascelles, despite his promise to the couple that marriage was not out of the question, began to back-pedal furiously. He realized that, whichever course of action was adopted in the long run, the Queen would necessarily be involved. Lascelles wanted to avoid this, especially so early in her reign. Within the royal household Princess Margaret's private affairs did not rank highly on the agenda of priorities, but, even so, Lascelles took it upon himself to make it known that friends of both the Princess and Townsend in royal service were neither to see nor to talk to them. In short, they were to be given the cold shoulder.

Princess Margaret's contempt for Sir Alan Lascelles grew from this time and in fact lasted until his death nearly thirty years later.

The Princess's love for Peter Townsend was not, of course, a matter which could be contained easily. It was no mere domestic issue. Consequently it fell to the Queen's Private Secretary to raise the matter with the Prime Minister, Winston Churchill. In turn Churchill contacted Sir Lionel Heald, the Attorney-General, who was asked to prepare a full report on the constitutional position and to seek, albeit informally, the views of Commonwealth leaders vis-à-vis a marriage between the Queen's sister and Peter Townsend. In the meantime Churchill promised Lascelles that, at his next meeting with the Queen, he too would press for Townsend's complete removal as the only decisive course of action. Impartiality, quite clearly, was to be found in very small measure.

More important than the personal feelings of either Lascelles or the Prime Minister was the Royal Marriages Act of 1772. Passed into statute by King George III, it was designed specifically to prevent undesirable marriages between the descendants of George II and such persons as might bring the crown into disrepute. Outmoded though it certainly appears nowadays, George III, as the father of several dissolute sons, had good reason to set his seal to it over two hundred years ago. In essence the Act prevented a royal marriage from taking place without the sovereign's consent. If such consent was withheld and the petitioning party was under twenty-five, he or she was obliged to wait. At the age of twenty-five, however, provided Parliament had received written notice – and neither House objected – the marriage could go ahead with or without the sovereign's assent.

Unfortunately, nobody explained the ramifications of this Act to Princess Margaret and in fact the constitutional position was only made really clear two years later, by which time the matter had reached monumental proportions and was being openly debated throughout the world.

It has been said that had the Queen's coronation not loomed so near, there might have been a more sympathetic response to Princess Margaret's situation, but, because of the timing, nobody wanted to become directly involved. On the other side of the Atlantic and indeed on the Continent, the coronation had already been eclipsed by stories of Princess Margaret's new romance. In itself the subject was hardly novel: since the age of nineteen the European press had claimed that the Princess was about to marry on no fewer than thirty-one occasions. This time, however, there was some authenticity in all that was being written.

In Britain the press remained silent, as it had during 1936 while its foreign brethren sizzled with talk of Edward VIII and Mrs Simpson. But, as in 1936, the silence could not be maintained indefinitely. A move might be made that the press would be unlikely to ignore. Unwittingly Princess Margaret made that move herself at Westminster Abbey following the coronation ceremony on 2 June. At its close, to quote Peter Townsend, 'a great crowd of crowned heads, of nobles and commons – and newspapermen, British and foreign – were gathered in the Great Hall. Princess Margaret came up to me; she looked superb, sparkling, ravishing. As we chatted she brushed a bit of fluff off my uniform. We laughed and thought no more of it. . . .'

For all its innocence, this gesture served to confirm all the rumours that had been buzzing around Fleet Street and well beyond for some time. The following day the Princess's action made headline news abroad, while at home it was contained for another eleven days. Then on 14 June, *The People* newspaper, under the guise of refuting foreign reports, squarely placed the cat among the pigeons. Under a banner headline 'The *People* Speaks Out', the story read:

> It is high time for the British public to be made aware of the fact that scandalous rumours about Princess Margaret are racing around the world. Newspapers in both Europe and America are openly asserting that the Princess is in love with a divorced man and that she wishes to marry him.
>
> Every newspaper which has printed the story names the man as Group Captain Peter Townsend, Equerry to the Queen and formerly Deputy Master of the Household ...

The story is of course utterly untrue. It is quite unthinkable that a Royal Princess, third in line of succession to the throne, should even contemplate a marriage with a man who has been through the divorce courts.

Group Captain Townsend was the innocent party in the divorce proceedings. It was he who secured a decree last year against his wife, Rosemary, on the grounds of adultery. She has since married John de Laszlo, son of the famous portrait painter.

But his innocence cannot alter the fact that a marriage between Princess Margaret and himself would fly in the face of Royal and Christian tradition. . . .

The morning after, Sir Alan Lascelles and Commander Richard Colville, the Queen's Press Secretary, advised Her Majesty that there was now no possibility that the rest of the national press would remain silent. Townsend *had* to go. Churchill again reiterated the same sentiment, while informing the Queen that the Cabinet, after unofficial talks on the subject, were unanimously against the marriage as, indeed, were the Commonwealth prime ministers. Moreover, though Princess Margaret herself was not to know it, it seemed unlikely that Parliament would approve the marriage even after she had attained her twenty-fifth birthday.

In the circumstances the only alternative would be to demand the ultimate sacrifice of the Princess. Were she to renounce the right of succession, not only for herself but for her heirs and descendants, and were she prepared to forfeit her Civil List income, then neither the Crown nor Parliament could prevent her from becoming Mrs Peter Townsend. Had Princess Margaret agreed to renounce her right of succession, together with her income of £6,000 under the Civil List, all Parliament needed to do was prepare a Special Act. Under the provisions of the Statute of Westminster, similar Acts would have been required of the Parliaments of Canada, New Zealand, Australia and South Africa.

Through all this the Group Captain's removal from Britain became daily closer. It was an inevitable step. The Princess and Peter Townsend had agreed that they must separate for the time being, though still looking towards marriage ultimately. Meanwhile, the Prime Minister issued firm instructions to the Air Minister: Lord de L'Isle, said Churchill, was to find an overseas posting for Townsend without delay.

On Tuesday 30 June 1953, at the start of a tour that had been planned for some time, Queen Elizabeth the Queen Mother and Princess Margaret boarded a B.O.A.C. Comet at Heathrow Airport bound for Salisbury, Rhodesia.

That morning, as Townsend recalled, 'the Princess was very calm for we felt certain of each other and, though it was hard to part, we were reassured by the promise, emanating from I know not where, but official, that my departure would be held over until her return on 17 July'.

Ahead of the Queen Mother and Princess Margaret lay a sixteen-day tour during which they would cover 1,500 miles by rail and road, in an area not toured by the Royal Family during the visit of 1947. They would take part in nine formal ceremonies of welcome, receive twenty-eight presentations of unspecified numbers of dignitaries and would inspect a dozen guards of honour in as many different locations. Fifty-four official engagements had been mapped out, most of them lasting between two and four hours, and during the full sixteen days, they were to be allowed a mere twenty-four hours to themselves.

On the morning of 8 July, the Queen Mother and her daughter arrived at the seven-year-old Leopard Rock Hotel in Umtali, set almost 5,000 feet above sea level and nestling luxuriously in the Vumba mountains. They had by now completed the first part of their visit. Princess Margaret, however, had hardly set foot inside the hotel before she left it to be flown to Salisbury and Government House with a temperature of 103°. She had succumbed to an attack of 'Bulawayo 'flu'. The Princess's illness coincided with news that Peter Townsend had received orders to quit Britain within seven days, just two days before the royal party was scheduled to return home.

Combining the two reports, stories circulated that Princess Margaret's problem was not 'flu but hysteria, that in the blackest of moods she had telephoned both the Queen and Townsend in London and that, when summoned, a doctor had prescribed tranquillizers. To put the record straight, the one call that Princess Margaret made was to the Queen, but only to let her know that she was ill with 'flu, and a doctor had of course been summoned to Government House, but only to treat her 'flu symptoms.

*   *   *

Of the three posts that had been offered to him – in Johannesburg, Singapore and Brussels – Peter Townsend had opted for the latter, accepting the post of Air Attaché at the British Embassy. Remonstrating with an immovable Sir Alan Lascelles, he pointed out that since he had only recently been awarded custody of his two young sons, he could hardly be expected to fly away to such far-flung places as South Africa or the Far East.

In Britain, reaction to this latest move provoked an outcry in the national press that was both loud and long. Writing in the independent socialist weekly *Tribune*, Michael Foot, the paper's editor, declared:

> *Tribune* believes that Princess Margaret should be allowed to make up her own mind whom she wants to marry. Most other people, we imagine, would agree with that simple proposition. But the British Cabinet does *not* agree ...
>
> The objection is based on the fact that Peter Townsend had been involved in a divorce case. That, in the view of the Church, is a reason for preventing him from marrying the Princess, even though Peter Townsend was an innocent party in the divorce action ...
>
> This intolerable piece of interference with a girl's private life is all part of the absurd myth about the Royal Family which has been so sedulously built up by interested parties in recent years. It recalls the hypocritical role played by the Church at the time of the Duke of Windsor's abdication.
>
> The incident is not made any more savoury by our knowledge that three members of the present Cabinet [Sir Anthony Eden, Sir Walter Monckton and Mr Peter Thorneycroft] have themselves been involved in divorce cases.
>
> The laws of England say that a man, whether he has divorced his wife or been divorced himself, is fully entitled to marry again. In some respects, those divorce laws are still too harsh. But no self-appointed busybody has the right to make them still harsher. If those laws are good they are good enough for the Royal Family.

In Southern Rhodesia on 12 July, Princess Margaret, having recovered both her health and her equilibrium, drove to Salisbury Station to meet her mother. The Queen Mother had travelled overnight from Fort Victoria and, together, they attended Divine Service in the Cathedral of St Mary and All Saints, which had been built sixty years earlier on the site of the thatched hut that had been the city's first church.

The following evening 'A Ball for Young People' was held at Government House in honour of Princess Margaret. Wearing a long dress of oyster-coloured tiered lace, together with a diamond tiara and necklace, her family orders and the recently-awarded G.C.V.O. (Grand Cross Victorian Order), the Princess was warmly greeted by one thousand guests as she entered the ballroom with her mother and the Governor, Sir John Kennedy.

Two days later the royal tour ended as it had begun, at Salisbury Airport, amid the cacophonous sounds of bellowed commands, the National Anthem, a salute of twenty-one guns and the cheers of onlookers.

CHAPTER SEVEN

A TIME FOR DECISIONS

In Brussels Peter Townsend made plans to fill the days of his exile purposefully. Having established himself in a small, comfortable flat on the Avenue Louise, he accepted a few invitations to social gatherings, mastered French and gave thought to a world tour. More immediately he improved the standard of his riding to enable him to participate in show jumping and was later admitted to the Etrier Belge, Belgium's most famous riding club. Within a few months he was building for himself a formidable reputation as a serious competitor in races throughout Europe.

While he and Princess Margaret got on with their lives, their story continued to simmer gently in newspaper offices where editors waited expectantly for the next episode. The wait was brief. Hardly had the Princess returned from Southern Rhodesia in July 1953, than an amendment to the 1937 Regency Act pushed her back on to the front pages. This amendment allowed for the Duke of Edinburgh, rather than Princess Margaret, to act as regent should the Queen die before Prince Charles reached manhood.

If it had hoped to pour oil on troubled waters, the Government of the day would have been better advised to think again about the timing of its announcement. Richard (Rab) Butler, acting Prime Minister during Winston Churchill's incapacity (he was gravely ill following a stroke), defended the release of the statement, telling the House of Commons that it had been under consideration for more than a year. The regency amendment, it was stressed, was not to be seen as the removal of one more obstacle from Princess Margaret's path to the altar, but rather the Queen's own wish that her husband

and not her sister should act as regent for the young Prince Charles in the event of her death.

With few exceptions the press thought it an unlikely story, and argued that the regency should be kept in the line of succession and not pass to someone (the Duke of Edinburgh) with no right of inheritance. *The Times*, however, approved the amendment, stating that the choice of 'understudy' was a matter for the Queen and her family to settle for themselves. The socialist *Tribune* entered the fray once more and asked, with a hint of sarcasm perhaps:

> Rub your eyes and read again. Haven't they got any history books at *The Times* office? Both the succession and the Regency are matters which Parliament has decided. . . . The best service the Government can do the Royal Family is to drop this Regency Bill. Indeed, the Regency Act of 1937 was passed for the express purpose of making the selections automatic and the controversies dead. So why dig them all up again?

Despite the eloquent arguments for leaving well alone and permitting Princess Margaret to assume the regency should the need arise, the Bill was pushed through both the Commons and the Lords early in November. It received Royal Assent on the 19th, just four days before the Queen and the new regent-designate set out on their six-month coronation tour of the Commonwealth.

Whatever Princess Margaret's private thoughts were about the amendment – and today she says that she always felt it was justified – the arguments soon blew over and were eventually forgotten.

During the following year Princess Margaret, who had been feeling 'rather blue' was roped into an amateur theatrical production for charity with which some of her friends were already involved. Not long before, the same company had produced *Lord and Lady Algy* in the West End. The play had not warranted the press coverage it received, but the response was sufficient to encourage the company in their ideas. Thus, in 1954, they decided to stage the Ian Hay-Edgar Wallace thriller *The Frog*.

The Queen raised no objections to her sister's participation and the Princess fell in with the plans, albeit 'cautiously'. It was an ideal distraction, filling her off-duty hours, while also allowing her to indulge one of her strongest interests, the theatre.

Billy Wallace was cast as a detective attempting to bring a terrorist brotherhood to justice, aided by Lord Porchester playing the part of a Cockney police Sergeant. The Duke of Devonshire accepted the role of prison governor and Raine Legge (today Countess Spencer) the part of the heroine – a night-club hostess. Princess Margaret's job as Assistant Director was to help keep the cast under control; it was thought that the players would be less likely to argue with her and would do what was asked promptly. Her friendship with Lord Glenconner, who was playing the title role and who, until now, had been no more than an acquaintance, grew from this time.

The Scala Theatre was booked for one week in June and, as soon as they returned from their tour, the Queen and the Duke of Edinburgh together with the Queen Mother attended one of the performances, impressed to learn that advance bookings already totalled £5,000. It was a staggering achievement for what the theatre's manager called 'a top-level amateur production'.

After the opening night, the cast gathered at the Milroy Club to relive each other's performances and to await the critics' verdicts in the early editions of the morning newspapers.

Noël Coward, who joined the first-night audience, was considerably less than impressed by what he had seen. A candid observer of everything, good, bad or indifferent, he noted in his diary:

> The whole evening was one of the most fascinating exhibitions of incompetence, conceit and bloody impertinence that I have ever seen in my life. With the exception of young Porchester, who at least tried to sustain a character, the entire cast displayed no talent whatsoever. Billy Wallace, the leading man, ambled on and off stage with his chin stampeding into his neck; nobody made the faintest effort to project their voices; Elsa Maxwell appeared in a cabaret scene and made a cracking ass of herself. Douglas Fairbanks [Jnr] played a small part in order, I presume, to prove that he was more one of 'them' than one of 'us'. . . .
>
> It was certainly a strong moral lesson for all of us never to be nervous again on opening nights. Those high-born characters we watched mumbling and stumbling about the stage are the ones who come to our productions and criticize us! They at least betrayed no signs of nervousness; they were unequivocally delighted with themselves from the first scene to the last, which, I may add, was a very long time indeed. In the dressing room afterwards, where we went civilly to congratulate Porchy, we found Princess Margaret eating *foie gras* sandwiches, sipping champagne and complaining that the audience laughed in the wrong places. We commiserated politely and left.

Among Princess Margaret's comments on Coward's diary entry was, 'I don't like *foie gras*.'

At the end of the play's brief run, Princess Margaret went on stage to thank the cast and to announce that the coffers of the Invalid Children's Aid Association (of which she is today President) would benefit to the tune of £10,000. 'It's been my lucky week,' she is alleged to have said, to the amusement of those who knew she had just won three-guineas' worth of books for correctly solving the crossword in the magazine *Country Life*.

The following month Princess Margaret became the first member of the Royal Family to visit Germany since the war. Moreover, the luncheon appointment she kept in Bonn with President Heuss and Chancellor Adenauer made her the first member of the British Royal Family to pay an official visit to a German head of state for more than forty years.

The purpose of her visit was to tour British military units, and during her four-day stay she inspected six army bases, one Royal Navy centre and three R.A.F. stations. At one of these she was invited to have a go at firing a 20-mm cannon from a jet fighter, and rose to the challenge.

One of the features of this visit that still stands out in the Princess's memory today, and one she least expected, was the number of people who waited to see her. 'I was met by enormous crowds,' she says, 'which surprised me so soon after the war.'

Also in hand at this time was Princess Margaret's first full-scale, official overseas tour in her own right. From 1 February to 2 March 1955, it was announced, Her Royal Highness would be visiting Trinidad, Grenada, St Vincent, Barbados, Antigua, St Kitts, Jamaica and the Bahamas. Almost inevitably there was talk in Britain that the tour's official status was a cover for a glossy, private Caribbean jaunt. Nor was such speculation much discouraged by a remark of the Queen's Press Secretary who said that, 'Her Royal Highness will, of course, shake hands with all of the considerable number of persons who are introduced to her.' Well might the Princess have made so small a concession had the tour been planned as a palm-fringed jamboree at the expense of the British taxpayer.

Trinidad, first claimed by Columbus for the Crown of Spain five hundred years earlier, welcomed the Princess with familiar cere-mony. The Governor of Trinidad and Tobago, Major-General Sir

Hubert Rance, in white uniform and plumed helmet, stepped forward to greet her and the ranks of the guard of honour stood rigidly to attention while the Princess fulfilled the obligatory inspection.

From Piarco Airport, the royal party drove slowly along the twenty-five-mile route to Government House, vividly dressed Trinidadians lining the roadside, and stopped briefly at the small township of Arima, the ancient home of the Caribs, the original inhabitants of the southern West Indies. There, local people had formed a queue on the parched race-track, waiting to be presented, while children in the 10,000-strong crowd provided a lusty and well-rehearsed rendering of *Land of Hope and Glory*.

The following day as the crowds grew larger – 100,000 waited outside Government House to watch her arrival at a garden party – the songs of welcome grew friendlier and more informal. 'With her beautiful blue eyes and curly hair, You'd know her for a Princess anywhere' ran the spontaneous doggerel of one calypso. 'Lovin' sister of Queen Lilibet, is Princess Margaret, she ent married, she ent tall, like to dance, like to sing, like to try out anything. If she been boy, she been king' was another. Both may, perhaps, have been 'composed' on the spur of the moment by the island's most famous calypso singer known by the unlikely name of 'Attila the Hun'.

A five-mile 'state' drive around the capital, standing in the back of an open car, so that she could be seen clearly, was followed by a visit to San Fernando, the 'town on stilts', where the Princess formally opened the San Fernando Colonial Hospital. On the way she had opened the new trunk road leading to the south of the island, naming it the 'Princess Margaret Highway'. Later Princess Margaret was treated to an incongruous display of Scottish country dancing performed by a group of West Indian girls.

The following day, as she flew across to Tobago (Robinson Crusoe's island) to complete a six-hour programme of engagements, it was pointed out to the Princess that a message had been daubed across the dark waters of the Great Pitch Lake. Flying low for a closer look, the whitewashed message read 'Have a good trip'.

Such was the genuine feeling that greeted Princess Margaret throughout her month-long tour that it left an indelible impression from which stemmed her desire to return to the West Indies more frequently. This desire was to be fulfilled many times over in the years ahead.

The press, both West Indian and British, wrote at length on the subject of the Princess and the 'spell' she cast over her hosts. In those less cynical days, nobody thought it necessary to lift the edge of the carpet to see if there was any dirt beneath, but a sobering insight into the attitudes of Government officials responsible for planning Princess Margaret's tour is provided by Noël Coward. He was staying in Kingston, Jamaica, as the guest of the Governor, Sir Hugh Foot, and his wife Sylvia, at the time of the visit and wrote in his diary:

> Apparently it has been laid down that on no account is she [Princess Margaret] to dance with any coloured person. This is, I think, a foolish edict . . . I should think that any presentable young Jamaican would be a great deal more interesting to dance with than the shambling Billy Wallace. The famous retrogressiveness of pompous English officialdom, like the 'old soldier' never dies; unfortunately it doesn't fade away either.

At the end of the Princess's stay, however, a less indignant Noël Coward wrote: 'Princess Margaret's visit has been a very great success and everybody says she has done it exceedingly well. On her last evening I drove to Port Antonio for her private "beach" party . . . which did *not* take place on the beach on account of wind and rain. . . . It was an extremely pleasant evening. She was sweet and gay and looked radiant.'

At home in Britain, the question of the Princess's proposed marriage was, as yet, no closer to being answered. At the end of the first year's wait requested by the Queen in 1953, a further year had been imposed. Now that second year had almost expired and the couple still had nothing to show for their patience.

Were those directly concerned with advising the Queen deliberately dragging their feet? Is it not possible that they believed Princess Margaret's twenty-fifth birthday might impose its own ultimatum, thus forcing her into exercising her right under the Royal Marriages Act? Be that as it may, speculation began to mount as her birthday drew closer, with a great many people fully expecting some kind of announcement about her future.

In early August, the Royal Family again migrated north to Scotland and keeping Princess Margaret company was Dominic Elliot, son of the Earl of Minto. By Sunday 21 August, three hundred newsmen were preparing to lay siege to Balmoral Castle. There had not been so much as a hopeful whisper from official sources, but the press intended to be on hand just in case, even though all the official statements indicated the normal family get-together. After breakfast the Princess was expected to open her birthday presents. Then, as usual, she and her family would attend church at nearby Crathie, and after this they were expected to have a picnic lunch. In the afternoon there was to be nothing more significant than the entire royal party's appearance at a local charity bazaar. There, in a wide, open marquee, they were all to assume the roles of sales assistants, lending a helping hand behind the counters.

A few weeks later, Sir Anthony Eden, who had succeeded Churchill as Prime Minister, arrived at Balmoral with his second wife, Clarissa. There was nothing unusual about the Prime Minister of the day being invited to spend a weekend with the sovereign, but this particular visit was invested with some importance. For Eden had to tell both the Queen and Princess Margaret that, in the opinion of the Cabinet, nothing had changed since 1953: the proposed marriage would not receive official sanction. If she intended to persist in her plans, said Eden, the only alternative would be for him to ask Parliament to pass a Bill which would necessarily deprive her (and her issue) of her rights of succession, her right to function as a Counsellor of State and her right to her income (which, in the case of an approved marriage, would be more than doubled to £15,000 per annum). The Prime Minister felt bound to say that he thought the whole issue would irreparably damage the standing of the Crown. In this, he said, he was firmly supported by the Marquess of Salisbury, Lord President of the Council and leader of the House of Lords. The Marquess of Salisbury, a High Anglican, had in fact threatened to resign from the Government rather than be responsible for passing a Bill that would permit Princess Margaret to marry a divorced man.

Ten days later on 12 October, an ebullient Princess Margaret travelled back to London. With her in one of the royal coaches attached to the Perth train were her lady-in-waiting, Lady Elizabeth Cavendish, her cousin, Princess Alexandra of Kent, and Lady Rose Baring, one of the Queen's ladies-in-waiting. The reason for the Princess's high spirits was soon revealed: Peter Townsend was also due to arrive in London that same day.

From Euston Station, Princess Margaret drove to Clarence House, while Townsend, who flew into Lydd Airport in Kent, drove to 19

Lowndes Square in Knightsbridge, where the Marquess of Aberga-venny, a close friend of the Royal Family, had put his flat at Townsend's disposal.

The following day the Hon. Jean Wills, one of Princess Margaret's Elphinstone cousins, lunched with Townsend at Lowndes Square before accompanying him on a much-publicized shopping spree in the West End. Then at 6.20 that evening, the Group Captain drove himself to Clarence House for his first 'official' meeting with Princess Margaret in two years. Timed from the moment he arrived to the moment he left by the ever watchful press corps, the couple were together for one hour and forty minutes.

Thus began the nineteen days in which public opinion grew more intense. Ninety-six per cent of the population, it was estimated, supported the Princess in her wish to marry the man of her choice. The Government fussed over the ins and outs of the Constitution, and the Church clucked about marriage and divorce, conveniently ignoring the fact that, as Townsend himself pointed out, 'The Church of England's "establishment" ... was itself founded on a divorce, that of Henry VIII and his Spanish wife, Catherine of Aragon'.

Media reports concerning every move made by Princess Margaret and Peter Townsend, and speculation about their plans for the future were relentless. So intense was the coverage that, as the Princess drove from Clarence House to Allanbay Park, the Berkshire estate of John and Jean Wills, on the afternoon of Friday 14 October, a statement was released from Buckingham Palace that said:

> In view of the varied reports which have been published, the Press Secretary to The Queen is authorised to say that no announcement concerning Princess Margaret's personal future is at present contem-plated. The Princess has asked the Press Secretary to express the hope that the press and public will extend to Her Royal Highness their customary courtesy and co-operation in respecting her privacy.

Such a request, however, had come rather too late in the day. The Princess's private life was now of such interest that the press could scarcely be expected to be called off the scent, leaving the world to wonder what was happening in the life of one of its most public figures.

As dusk fell that Friday evening, Princess Margaret's black

Rolls-Royce with its distinctive number plate PM 6450 sped into the driveway of Allanbay Park. Behind her the gates were slammed shut and a police car positioned firmly in front of them. The Chief Constable of Berkshire personally masterminded the security blanket which was thrown over the house and its fifty acres. Inside the grounds a police dog and its handler patrolled the perimeter of the estate, while more police circled outside. Six patrol cars cruised the surrounding lanes of Binfield and radio-monitored officers around the house ensured that none of the press waiting at the gates gained admittance.

Townsend himself had arrived two hours earlier and, with the exception of Princess Margaret's attendance at church that Sunday at the Royal Chapel of All Saints in Windsor Great Park, the couple did not move from Allanbay. It was said that one French magazine had offered the Wills's butler £1,000 for 'inside' information, but the offer was flatly declined. Bribery came much cheaper, however, where the innocent young daughter of the house was concerned: seven-year-old Marilyn Wills, the Princess's god-daughter, was offered one pound and some chocolate to tell what she knew. It only happened once. When discovered, this small crack in the security system was closed, though, as might have been expected, Marilyn had nothing of any importance to tell.

During the next few days a succession of friends such as the Michael Brands, the John Lowthers and the Mark Bonham Carters offered the couple their hospitality: first dinner and then an hour or two in which they were left quietly to themselves.

By now the issue had even reached a stage where a few familiar jokes were being made about it. In one radio programme, for instance, a B.B.C. comedian, asking his stooge to read the day's news, was told: 'They had tea together again.' And *Punch* magazine, whose editor Malcolm Muggeridge was no lover of royalty, ran a cartoon of a contemplative child counting peas on her dinner-plate. The caption read, 'Tinker, Tailor, Soldier, Group Captain'.

Almost inevitably the mood of the nation closely resembled that of December 1936. For just as the Duke of Windsor's popularity appeared boundless at that moment of crisis, so at this crucial time in her life did Princess Margaret's.

'I certainly wish her great happiness if she marries him,' said the Duchess of Windsor, who knew only too well the might of the establishment's opposition, as well as the force of public opinion. Gladys Townsend's plea for her son was more plaintive. 'All I want is to see Peter happy again,' she said. Even Willie Hamilton MP, who from behind his protective screen of parliamentary privilege was to earn notoriety for his criticism of the Royal Family and especially of Princess Margaret, found a few favourable words: 'The Church of England is the opposition to the marriage,' he claimed. 'They are trying to tell her whom she should marry. It is fantastic.'

Equally fantastic was the way in which the episode continued to monopolize the prime spreads of the country's newspapers. Normally reluctant to join in the mêlée with its less scrupulous colleagues, *The Times* published its own thoughts on the matter:

> Now in the twentieth century conception of the monarchy the Queen has come to be the symbol of every side of life of this society, its universal representative in whom her people see their better selves ideally reflected; and since part of their ideal is of family life, the Queen's family has its own part in the reflection. If the marriage which is now being discussed comes to pass, it is inevitable that this reflection becomes distorted. The Princess will be entering into a union which vast numbers of her sister's people, all sincerely anxious for her lifelong happiness, cannot in conscience regard as a marriage. This opinion would be held whether the Church of England were established or not, and extends to great bodies of Christians outside it. That devout men have argued that it is a wrong interpretation of Christianity is not here relevant. All that matters is that it is widely and sincerely held; and therefore that a royal marriage which flouted it would cause acute division among loyal subjects everywhere. . . .
>
> If the Princess finally decides, with all the anxious deliberation that clearly she has given to her problem, that she is unable to make the sacrifice involved in her continued dedication to her inherited part, then she has a right to lay down a burden that is too heavy for her. . . .
>
> But the peoples of the Commonwealth would see her step down from her high place with the deepest regret, for she has adorned it, and is everywhere honoured and loved. . . . These things said, the matter is, in the last resort, one to be determined solely by Princess Margaret's conscience.

The *Daily Mirror*, which was soon to demand a decision of the Princess under a banner headline urging 'Come on Margaret!', asked in response to *The Times* leader, 'Would *The Times* have preferred this vivacious young woman to marry one of the witless wonders with whom she has been hobnobbing these past few years? Or to live her life in devoted spinsterhood?'

The press argued backwards and forwards, attacking the sterile arrogance of the Church and the pomposity of the Government, while Princess Margaret and Peter Townsend gradually found their own answer. There can never be any doubt about their love, but it seemed that each new move brought with it fresh disappointment. Consequently, as the Princess herself now explains, both Townsend and she felt thoroughly drained, thoroughly demoralized. They had reached a stage, in fact, where they could look at what lay before them dispassionately. This was the moment for Townsend to bow out of the Princess's life. He would not and could not ask her to marry him, he said. The sacrifices demanded of her would be far too great. They would almost certainly ruin her – and for what? In all conscience, the Group Captain said, he was not prepared to take her away from the only kind of life she knew. The future was too uncertain.

In his memoirs, Peter Townsend wrote of his meeting with Princess Margaret during the evening of 22 October: 'We were both exhausted, mentally, emotionally, physically. We felt mute and numbed at the centre of this maelstrom.'

Princess Margaret spent the following day with the Queen and the Duke of Edinburgh at Windsor Castle, from where, 'in great distress', she telephoned Townsend. 'She did not say what had passed between herself and her sister and brother-in-law,' he wrote, 'but doubtless, the stern truth was dawning on her.'

By the time the couple met at Clarence House the next evening, the realization that marriage was impossible, that, in the words of Peter Townsend, it was a 'no deal situation' had finally hit them. It was now that they sat down together to draft a statement. They worked at it until they were both satisfied that it stressed not only the futility of the situation but the resignation of their feelings: 'For a few moments we looked at each other; there was a wonderful tenderness in her eyes which reflected, I suppose, the look in mine. We had reached the end of the road.'

The first person to be told of the couple's decision was the Archbishop of Canterbury. As the Princess entered his study at Lambeth Palace, Dr Fisher reached for a book on a nearby shelf.

'You can put away your books Archbishop,' the Princess said. 'I am not going to marry Peter Townsend. I wanted you to know first.'

Dr Fisher sat quietly and listened as Princess Margaret told him why she and Peter Townsend had decided to surrender their hopes of a life together. At the end, he said, rejoicing, 'What a wonderful person the Holy Spirit is.'

Four days later, and one week after it had been drawn up, the Princess's statement was finally released to the world. Dated Monday 31 October 1955, the communiqué read:

> I would like it to be known that I have decided not to marry Group Captain Townsend. I have been aware that, subject to my renouncing my rights of succession, it might have been possible for me to contract a civil marriage. But mindful of the Church's teachings that Christian marriage is indissoluble, and conscious of my duty to the Commonwealth, I have resolved to put these considerations before others. I have reached this decision entirely alone and in doing so I have been strengthened by the unfailing support and devotion of Group Captain Townsend. I am deeply grateful for the concern of all those who have constantly prayed for my happiness.

The supreme irony of Princess Margaret's decision in 1955 would not be realized for another twenty-three years, when the Princess herself became – albeit reluctantly – a divorcée.

CHAPTER EIGHT

ANTONY ARMSTRONG-JONES

Though the public had no way of knowing it, relief and resignation, rather than anger or sorrow, were the paramount emotions experienced by Princess Margaret and Peter Townsend as 1955 drew to a close. Townsend returned to Brussels that autumn while the Princess continued to fulfil her engagements, public as well as private, with a lighter heart than many would have believed possible.

It has been claimed, rather fancifully, that Princess Margaret locked herself away in her rooms at Clarence House, pining for Townsend and refusing to see even her closest friends. Such a romantic image is, however, far from the truth, although at this time public sympathy enveloped the Princess to such an extent that she could have behaved in that way, or in any other way she pleased and not have met with criticism. Fleet Street beat its breast, entreating others to do likewise, but among those who managed to keep some kind of perspective was, once again, Noël Coward, who wrote in his diary: 'She can't know, poor girl, being young and in love, that love dies soon and that a future with two strapping stepsons and a man eighteen years older than herself would not really be very rosy.... At least she hasn't betrayed her position and her responsibilities and that is arid comfort for her with half the world religiously exulting and the other half pouring out a spate of treacly sentimentality.' Then, on a note which clearly spoke of society's double standards, Coward put away his pen: 'I hope that they had the sense to hop into bed a couple of times at least, but this I doubt.'

Whether Princess Margaret and Peter Townsend would have been happy is a matter of conjecture. With the benefit of hindsight, however, the Princess has her doubts. For his part, Peter Townsend was to say many years later: 'She could have married me only if she'd been prepared to give up everything. I simply hadn't the weight, I knew it, to counterbalance all she would have lost. Thinking of it calmly ... you couldn't have expected her to become an ordinary housewife overnight, could you? And to be fair, I wouldn't have wanted that for her.'

Now, at the end of 1955, the couple had to come to grips with organizing their separate lives. For Townsend, this meant the realization of a round-the-world tour, no doubt designed to escape as far away as possible from the hypocrisy of the British establishment. Planned with the 'precision of a military operation', he set to work mapping out an eighty-week journey in which, by car, he would visit sixty countries and cover 60,000 miles. He intended to start out in September 1956.

Princess Margaret herself, though feeling no urge to escape, was also to leave Britain that September, on a tour of East Africa. And while those concerned with planning the tour busied themselves with details, the rest of the Princess's diary for 1956 began to fill rapidly. In June she made her first visit abroad when, together with her uncle Henry, Duke of Gloucester, Vice-Patron of the British Olympic Association, the Princess flew to Sweden where the Olympic equestrian events were being held. There, she and her uncle joined the Queen and the Duke of Edinburgh, who had just completed a state visit to Sweden's King Gustav VI Adolf, who also happened to be Prince Philip's uncle by marriage.

Earlier in the year at St Martin's Theatre in London's West End a new revue had opened, staged by the innovative choreographer John Cranko. Called *Cranks*, it was a production with which Lady Elizabeth Cavendish, a friend of Cranko and one of Princess Margaret's closest friends, had become involved. A magistrate and sister of the present Duke of Devonshire, Lady Elizabeth was one of the Princess's earliest ladies-in-waiting and it was now with her that Princess Margaret watched and thoroughly enjoyed one of the show's rehearsals. Lady Elizabeth also managed to engage another of her friends to provide the house photographs; he was an up-and-coming photographer called Antony Armstrong-Jones.

The Princess and 'the Jones boy' as some were later to call him did not meet at this time. Nor – as some have claimed – did their paths cross two months later, when Armstrong-Jones acted as official photographer at the wedding of two of Princess Margaret's friends, Lord Glenconner and Lady Anne Coke, the elder daughter of the Earl and Countess of Leicester. In fact the Princess asked many years later, 'Did Tony take the photographs?'

With most of her friends now married, or at least seriously involved in relationships, Princess Margaret felt inclined to think that she herself would never follow suit. During the 1950s there seemed to be a marked trend towards early marriages and in 1956, as the Princess approached her twenty-sixth birthday, it was beginning to look as though she would find herself in a similar position to that of her late great-aunt Toria. The second of Edward VII's three daughters, Princess Victoria was never allowed to marry, despite proposals from a member of the Baring family and even from the Prime Minister of the day, Lord Rosebery. Queen Alexandra, however, steadfastly and selfishly refused to consider the possibility of her daughter marrying. The result was that Toria remained at home as her mother's companion, growing old before her time and seeking solace in illness, both real and imagined.

Parallels between great-aunt and great-niece would certainly have been drawn by historians had Princess Margaret remained single. But what was not to become public knowledge for many years was the Princess's acceptance of the one man among her closest friends who had wanted to marry her for some time.

Billy Wallace, a grandson of the distinguished architect Sir Edwin Lutyens, had sought Princess Margaret's hand several times and had been gently rejected. In 1956, however, it was a different story. Believing it was better to marry 'somebody one at least liked', rather than face a long, lonely spinsterhood, the Princess agreed to marry Wallace on condition that their engagement received the Queen's blessing. Naturally he readily agreed to this proviso and, having convinced himself that it would be no more than a few months before he could plight his troth before the entire world, he went to the Bahamas for some much needed sunshine after a recent illness. It was while there, however, that he had a brief holiday romance. So confident was he that nothing could prevent him from becoming engaged to Princess Margaret that, upon his return, he regaled her with the details of his holiday. When the Princess promptly left him, Wallace was astonished.

It was not until 1965, five years after the Princess herself had married, that Billy Wallace, plagued by ill health (he died twelve years later of cancer), found a wife in the Honourable Elizabeth Hoyer-Millar, elder daughter of Lord Inchyra. By that time, Princess Margaret had long forgiven him and accepted his invitation to the wedding.

Throughout the summer of 1956, Princess Margaret spent a good deal of time brushing up her knowledge of the countries she was about to visit as part of her East African tour, which covered not only Britain's East African and Indian Ocean territories but also Mauritius, Zanzibar, Tanganyika and Kenya. The latter was technically the most challenging stop of all, for only two years earlier the atrocities of the Mau-Mau had hung over a country rife with anti-British propaganda. The Princess was noted for her ability to bring people together, but she would need all the tact and diplomacy at her command.

As reports home indicated, Princess Margaret proved the perfect antidote to all the anti-British rancour of the recent past and excelled herself in soothing troubled waters. This tour – like so many more to follow – was doubtless remembered by the Princess as a series of indistinct images of official receptions, ceremonial drives through streets jammed with effusive crowds, tribal gatherings, formal addresses, garden parties and endless presentation lines. Such are the formalities which face visiting royalty, but the Princess overcame any potential stuffiness by showing an interest and enthusiasm which frequently left colonial bureaucrats of the old school dazed.

In Zanzibar the Princess paid a ceremonial call on the seventy-eight-year-old Sultan to pass on her sister's felicitations. The world's longest-reigning sovereign, the Sultan of Zanzibar had occupied his throne since 1911. With thrones in mind, it was hoped that when Princess Margaret attended what was described as a 'tribal gymkhana' in Tanganyika, she might be seated in the very same chair from which, some thirty years earlier, her uncle David, as Prince of Wales, had watched a similar gathering. But this carved 'throne', stored for so long in a thatched hut, had fallen prey to damp and white ants. Against such considerable opposition very little of it remained, 'Which decisively proves', the Governor, Sir Edward Twining, allegedly remarked, 'that people in grass houses shouldn't stow thrones.'

In Tanganyika there was also a chance meeting for the Princess with the man who, under more favourable circumstances, would have become her brother-in-law. He was Peter Townsend's younger brother, Francis. Stationed in Arusha as the British District Commissioner and heading a deputation of Masai warriors, the younger Townsend's meeting with Princess Margaret was necessarily short and formal. But if, as has been said, some people were thrown into a quandary by his presence, the Princess herself saw no good reason why he should not be presented or indeed why he should not be acknowledged.

To all those who came into contact with her, it was clear that Princess Margaret had now put the Townsend issue well behind her. She was enjoying herself in a natural, down-to-earth manner while proving again that British royalty need not be regarded as a cliché from an imperial past. In fact there was nothing clichéd, or even predictable, about the Princess who was, according to Louis Armstrong, 'one hip chick'.

This was the era of rock 'n' roll, when girls wore pony-tails and swirling skirts, while their partners sported drain-pipe trousers and well-oiled hair. Jazz, too, was as popular in England as it was in America, and Princess Margaret was as much a fan of all this as she was a devotee of the more classical art forms. Twice in one day, for example, she drove to the Royal Festival Hall to attend concerts given by Count Basie. The cinema, in keeping with modern trends, also offered 'rock' entertainment and the Princess went to see the most popular films of this kind on the circuit.

'I was rockin' and rollin' with Princess Margaret last night,' wrote American journalist Robert Musel in his *Boston Traveler* column on 15 February 1957, 'and may I tell cats everywhere that this royal chick is cool, real cool. We were neighbors at a rock and roll film *The Girl Can't Help It*, which stars Jayne Mansfield. When I happened to see the Princess hopping out of a Rolls-Royce in front of the cinema, I followed close behind. One of the features of the film is a series of rock 'n' roll acts ... the guitar strummers, the blues shouters, the pianists beating out persistent 12-bar phrases. The Princess hopped in her seat. An usherette reported that she also took off her shoes, propped her feet on a railing and wiggled her toes in time with the music.'

From another film, *Rock Around the Clock*, a new 'in' expression was culled, one which popular legend maintains was used by the Princess to bewildering effect during her visit to Kenya. Taking formal leave of his royal guest, the Governor, Sir Evelyn Baring, was said to have been left high and dry by Princess Margaret's off-the-cuff remark, 'See you later alligator.' An aide advised the Governor that the correct response, should Her Royal Highness say it again, was, 'In a while crocodile.' Alas, the Princess assures one that the story is apocryphal.

Nonetheless Princess Margaret 'swung' with the rest of her generation, keeping up with the popular sounds. At Clarence House she and her friends enjoyed endless record sessions, invariably settling themselves on the floor of her sitting-room. To her collection of records she added those of her favourite guitarist Josh White and her favourite singer Ella Fitzgerald. A little later, albums by Cleo Laine, whom the Princess also greatly admires, were avidly bought.

Back in England from her African tour, the majority of Princess Margaret's official engagements were connected with the presidencies and patronages she had accepted or which, at the start of her career, had been accepted for her by the King and Queen. To this steadily growing list were added several honorary appointments within the armed services. By 1956, for example, she had been appointed Colonel-in-Chief of Queen Alexandra's Royal Army Nursing Corps, The Highland Light Infantry, and the Suffolk Regiment. Overseas, the Princess was Colonel-in-Chief of the Highland Light Infantry of Canada, the Women's Royal Australian Army Corps, the Northland Regiment (Royal New Zealand Infantry Corps) and the Rand Light Infantry. During the next few years Princess Margaret also assumed further service appointments, and her knowledge of and her pride in her regiments belie churlish claims that war games, inspections and regimental life have always bored her.

Towards the end of 1956 Princess Margaret gave fifteen sittings to Pietro Annigoni, whose famous portrait of the Queen ('the Blue Portrait' as it is known today, because of the predominant colouring) had been completed the previous year. Annigoni said that he had wanted to paint the Princess from the time he first saw her in Italy seven years earlier. In 1957 the finished canvas, which was the object of much comment, was hung at the Royal Academy. Today the portrait hangs in the entrance hall of Princess Margaret's home at Kensington Palace. One of Annigoni's preliminary sketches, however, is occasionally displayed publicly as part of the Royal Collection.

Eighteen months after he had set out on his world tour, and two and a half years after Princess Margaret's statement was released, Peter Townsend returned to London.

'The man with whom I shook hands', wrote Townsend's biographer, Norman Barrymaine, in 1958, 'was very different from the man to whom I had bidden farewell. Peter was now bronzed and fit; his eyes had a new alertness and there was a determination about him which I had not seen since those far-off days of the Battle of Britain.'

To Barrymaine and, indeed, to the press at large Townsend's reappearance and Princess Margaret's carefree mood, now often remarked upon, could mean only one thing: that the question of marriage was again in the air. The couple had tea together at Clarence House on 28 March and hardly had Townsend arrived than the evening newspapers were boldly proclaiming, 'They're Together Again'. It was a brief, harmless meeting, but one which caused a furore because the Queen was paying a State Visit to the Netherlands and was said not to have known in advance of Townsend's visit.

Yet again press invention ran riot and, according to reports, the Princess and her sister were at loggerheads. So quickly did fresh stories escalate that Townsend felt bound to issue a statement of his own. In it he said: 'There are no grounds whatever for supposing that my seeing Princess Margaret in any way alters the situation declared specifically in the Princess's statement in the autumn of 1955.' The following day, the Princess flew off on an official visit to the Highland Light Infantry stationed in Germany, while Peter Townsend drove to Somerset to visit his mother.

There were to be no further meetings for Princess Margaret and the Group Captain, despite the fact that a warm friendship existed and continued to exist between them for several more years. 'We had an understanding that if Peter was here he should come in,' the Princess says, 'but it soon became obvious that that would never work.'

Official engagements were in any case taking up most of Princess Margaret's time in 1958, which proved to be one of the busiest years since the start of her public career a full decade before. In April she visited British Guiana, British Honduras and Trinidad, where she inaugurated the Legislature of the new West Indies Federation (destined to be short-lived, as the Princess herself had privately, but accurately predicted). In July she visited British Columbia to attend the provincial centenary celebrations before embarking on a tour of other parts of Canada; and two month later, she was in Belgium to visit the Brussels Expo '58.

Between her overseas engagements and those which kept her on the move at home, the Princess finally met Antony Armstrong-Jones. On 20 February 1958 they were both guests of Lady Elizabeth Cavendish at a private dinner party in Cheyne Walk, Chelsea. Antony Armstrong-Jones was good company: charming, talented, full of energy and, with his fair hair, blue eyes and slight build, physically attractive. Princess Margaret and he were intrigued by one another but, contrary to some claims, their feelings did not amount to love at first sight. In fact they might never have met again had it not been for a particularly close friend of Princess Margaret's who asked if she would have a new set of photographs taken especially for him by Armstrong-Jones. From the resulting second meeting the couple began to warm to each other.

Tony, as he was always known, was born in London on 7 March 1930. His father, Ronald Armstrong-Jones, was educated at Eton and at Magdalen College, Oxford. A barrister of some note at the time of his son's birth, he was later elevated to the rank of Queen's Counsel. Tony's mother was Ronald's first wife, Anne, daughter of Lieutenant-Colonel Leonard Messel, whose son Oliver, became the celebrated theatrical designer. Anne Messel married Armstrong-Jones in July 1925, but the marriage was dissolved nine years later when their son was four.

Tony's father subsequently married twice more, first Carol Coombe, an Australian actress, and then Jenifer Unite, an air hostess.

His mother also remarried. Her second husband, four years her junior and, because of his good looks, nicknamed 'the Adonis of the peerage', was Michael Parsons, Earl of Rosse, the owner of estates both in England and Ireland. One of the largest of these, comprising 26,500 acres, was Birr in County Offaly; and it was between this attractive seventeenth-century castle with its famous box-hedge gardens and Womersley Park in South Yorkshire that Antony Armstrong-Jones spent much of his childhood.

Sandroyd preparatory in Surrey was his first school, followed by Eton. As he was packed off for his first term at boarding school, Armstrong-Jones senior told him, 'You will be getting a great many letters, but don't bother answering them unless you feel like it, except those from Birr [his mother and stepfather], Nymans [the home of his Messel grandparents in Sussex] and myself.'

Academically, Tony Armstrong-Jones was far from outstanding; indeed in one end-of-term report a master remarked curtly, 'Maybe he is interested in some subject, but it isn't a subject we teach here.' That photography – one of his keenest interests – was not to be found on the Eton curriculum scarcely deterred him from pursuing it to the best of his ability, if to the detriment of everything else. His first efforts, however, were not considered too highly. 'I never thought he would make a photographer. He was too impetuous,' said the local chemist near Birr, who had tried to teach him the science of printing and developing. The mother of his first model, the chemist's assistant, is said to have been more forthright in her judgement, remarking, 'We thought his pictures were daft.' The day had yet to come, of course, when the signature 'Snowdon' was as good, if not better, than that of the acknowledged master of photography Cecil Beaton.

At one point it looked as though Tony was to have no future of any description, whether in photography or anything else, for while staying with his father at Plâs Dinas, near Caernarvon in North Wales, he was struck down by what was thought to be tubercular meningitis. Summoned immediately to Plâs Dinas, Tony's mother turned in desperation to her brother after being told that hope for her teenage son's recovery had all but been abandoned. Oliver Messel immediately recommended his own doctor, Sir Henry (later Lord) Cohen. At this time the distinguished physician was based in Liverpool and it was to his hospital there that Tony was taken by ambulance in a ninety-mile emergency dash. The disease was, in fact, polio and although Armstrong-Jones eventually recovered, having spent more than a year in a wheelchair, he was left with one leg slightly shorter than the other.

Given that his academic prowess as a student at Eton had earned him no laurels and that his illness had then disrupted his education, it seems extraordinary that Tony succeeded in being admitted to Jesus College, Cambridge to read Natural Sciences. Once there, he changed direction and chose Architecture instead, following in the footsteps of his German great-uncle, Alfred Messel, who designed the Berlin National Gallery.

In the event, the tranquillity of his rooms in Chapel Court overlooking the quad and the ancient chapel did not suit Armstrong-Jones's temperament. Not for him the peace necessary for study, nor, as it transpired, the School of Architecture in Scroope Terrace. As soon as it was discovered that he had some rowing experience, he was pushed into training as a cox for the Cambridge Eight, and the river and photography soon began to claim his time and energy and all other hopes faded quietly away.

Cambridge did, however, offer Armstrong-Jones his first job as a photographer, working for *Varsity*, the undergraduate newspaper. The general reaction to his work was once again far from encouraging; it was, in fact, savage. Yet criticism only served to harden his resolve to succeed.

By contacting a number of magazines of the type that carefully chronicle the lives of those who spend their time hunting and shooting, he received commissions to cover various sporting and social activities. Though hardly an inspiration to others, his work was published and this at least transformed him from an amateur to a professional photographer. With this modest achievement to his credit, even if it was not what had been expected of him, Armstrong-Jones was about to be sent down. He was not surprised to learn that the School of Architecture had pronounced him a failure.

In a letter to his mother in which he confessed that he had failed his examinations, Tony explained that he had often considered photography as a profession and now he wanted to see if he could make it work. The response from Lady Rosse came by return. Her telegram read 'Do not agree suggestion changing career.'

Nonetheless Tony was given his head and, no matter how much his mother might have wanted him to become an architect, both she and his father agreed to do all they could to help him in his new career. With an introduction from his stepmother (at that time Carol Coombe) and with a fee paid by his father, Tony Armstrong-Jones joined the studio of Henry Nahum, who was better known as Baron, a photographer of royalty and high society, and a friend of the Duke of Edinburgh. Six months later, Tony branched out on his own with the help of £1,000 given him by his father. After a brief spell in other premises, he moved into 20 Pimlico Road. In what had been an ironmonger's shop, next door to the Sunlight Laundry and beneath a rather dilapidated block of Victorian flats, Armstrong-Jones set to work.

He turned the ground floor into his studio, while the smaller basement area became his home, furnished with eye-catching bits and pieces he had picked up along the way, including a mirror on which his guests were invited to scrawl their names with a sharp-edged diamond kept expressly for that purpose. Linking the studio with the room downstairs was a spiral staircase which he designed himself.

As a professional photographer, Armstrong-Jones undertook all the work he could get, but his particular interest was in the theatre. Quite apart from his family connexions, his was the world of the stage arts, and from it came many of his friends. The Royal Court Theatre in Sloane Square, which lies a few minutes away from 20 Pimlico Road, proved one of the first outlets for his talents as a theatrical photographer. If the Royal Court's productions were innovative, so too were Tony's action studies of the casts in rehearsal. In fact his was a style that was soon to be widely copied by theatres in the West End.

Theatrical photography, however, paid badly and he began to turn his sights elsewhere – to the more moneyed world of fashion. Here he struck up a happy and fairly lucrative association with *Vogue* magazine, tried his hand at fashion designing and then leapt into advertising. This, too, proved successful as his campaign for *Queen* magazine, owned by a friend, Jocelyn Stevens, bore testimony.

By now the fashionable world was fast becoming Tony's special oyster, and he soon found his way into the even more tantalizing world of princes. He photographed the young Duke of Kent, who decked himself out in military regalia in the studio at Pimlico Road, and he trundled his photographic equipment along to Buckingham Palace. There he took semi-formal studies of the Queen's children, Prince Charles and Princess Anne, and before long he was asked back to photograph the Queen herself.

The talent and energy that underlay this success story went with a gregarious and extrovert personality of considerable charm that was obviously an attraction to those he met in his work and socially. This charm has been described as calculating; he could, it is said, 'soft-soap skilfully'. And a friend from these early years of his career says that kindness was not a major characteristic of his; another says even that it did not exist in him at all. Yet this is also the man who has always shown concern for, among other causes, the welfare of the disabled – he had after all come perilously near to leading the life of a cripple himself.

To Princess Margaret, Tony represented a complete change from all the Lords, the Honourables and the traditionally acceptable people with whom she had always socialized. He was not completely without the right type of background, but he was, to all intents and purposes, a part of the working population with which royalty did not, either by choice or convention, associate freely. With no private wealth to speak of, he worked to earn his living. Moreover, with his sometimes *outré* apparel and his bohemian life-style – not to mention the colourful diversity of his friends – he was a non-conformist, putting little store by rank, background or what was or what was not considered 'acceptable'.

Over twenty years later he was to say, 'I enjoy every second of life. I'm a sort of gypsy, I suppose.' It was precisely this kind of spirit which aroused the 'gypsy' in Princess Margaret, for in some ways she doubtless saw her friendship with Armstrong-Jones as an assertion of her own individuality. After all, nobody, not even a member of the Royal Family, can inhabit a small, exclusive world without occasionally wondering about life beyond. This was perhaps best summed-up by Jocelyn Stevens when he said of Princess Margaret, 'I have always regarded her as a bird in a gilded cage. She would have loved to break free, but was never able to.'

Armstrong-Jones's way of life and his dislike of formality did not exclude the 'correct' attitude in his response to Princess Margaret, a respect not simply for the Princess as a person, but for all she represented. He called her 'Ma'am' and was careful not to err in the direction of over-familiarity.

If it is true that part of the joy of falling in love lies in the discovery of one another's interests, then the Princess and Tony Armstrong-Jones clearly delighted in finding each other, for they stood, in many respects, on common ground. The theatre, for example, is an abiding passion of them both and so, too, is the ballet (only a year before their meeting, Princess Margaret had accepted the presidency of the Royal Ballet Company). They were at home among the witty and the clever, and in return both excelled as conversationalists and raconteurs.

Armstrong-Jones the designer also discovered, perhaps to his surprise, Princess Margaret the artist. In this respect the Princess possesses what she calls 'certain talents' which may be seen at their best 'when the Muse inspires me'. There are, for instance, floral pictures meticulously worked in coloured feathers, and in particular a tea service of cobalt-blue porcelain painted with a design of vertical white quill feathers and stamped with her personal monogram, the initial M beneath a royal coronet. 'I also once composed a lament, words as well as music,' the Princess says. 'That was after Peter Townsend and I knew we couldn't get married.'

The only one of Princess Margaret's interests which Tony could never share was music – he is tone deaf. The Princess, on the other hand, possesses appreciable musical talents, both as a pianist and as a singer; in any other walk of life, it has often been said, the Princess could have become a concert pianist or a professional singer. This is an exaggeration by the media in the same way that Princess Margaret's talents as an actress have been exaggerated, and she does not take such statements at face value. The truth is that, while the Princess is an accomplished pianist, she is happier playing for her own amusement or accompanying herself when singing. Of her high soprano voice, however, she was justly proud. 'I was able to hit F above high C,' she says.

Her abilities as a mimic have not been overlooked by writers either, yet her talent here lies not so much in her ability to impersonate as to assume one of a range of authentic accents or dialects. Her style could, perhaps, be compared to that of the late Joyce Grenfell. Indeed it is interesting to note that Princess Margaret and Mrs Grenfell (who was a niece of Nancy, Lady Astor) once agreed that they shared a talent 'to do types' of people, rather than to impersonate given individuals. Like the actress, the Princess might, for example, relate a conversation she has overheard by 'doing' – not impersonating – the type of person involved.

CHAPTER NINE

A ROOM AND BEYOND

Through her presidency of the Dockland Settlement and her involvement in charities concerned with child welfare, Princess Margaret was no stranger to London's East End. Yet because it was a far cry from the mansions and elegant terraces of smart Mayfair, Kensington and Chelsea, it was not considered the type of place an off-duty Princess would normally be found. 'That's only what the snobs thought,' the Princess says, but it was precisely this attitude which allowed her to visit Bermondsey, an area to which she became fondly attached, without feeling the need for any form of disguise.

It was in Bermondsey during the late 1950s that William Glenton, an acquaintance of Antony Armstrong-Jones who was working as a journalist, had a small terraced house. Three hundred years old and backing straight on to the Thames, 59 Rotherhithe Street was eventually demolished because, said the local authority dismissively, it was 'artisan', of no interest and no value. For some time before the bulldozers moved in, however, the house provided a private retreat – later described by the press as a 'love-nest' – for Princess Margaret and Armstrong-Jones.

Author Mark Girouard located it 'down in the Pool, where the river is at its most wonderful, romantic and extraordinary ... there is no embankment, no traffic, no noise, except the occasional unearthly bellowing of a ship's hooter; the houses look straight out across the moored barges, the tugs and the occasional great ship, to a tangled skyline of cranes ...'

Having persuaded Bill Glenton to rent the ground-floor room to him, Tony Armstrong-Jones was in his element making it habitable after years of neglect. He had not taken it on with a view to leaving Pimlico Road, but simply as an alternative 'home', in much the same way that his wealthier friends and contacts left London for weekends in their country houses.

There are limits to what can be achieved by way of decoration in a relatively small room, but the simplicity of the finished decor in Tony's East End room was of a style that would appeal to thousands of young people setting up home for the first time. The walls were painted white, beams were scrubbed and, where water-pipes intruded, Tony built pine cupboards to conceal them. On the floor was laid rush-matting and the furniture was simple and unpretentious: a deal table, a number of easy chairs, a corner china cabinet, and an upright piano.

When it was complete and Tony was ready to entertain, one of his first invitations was received by Princess Margaret. For her, the 'little white room', as it became known, held a special fascination. 'It had the most marvellous view,' she recalls. 'One walked into the room and there was the river straight in front. At high tide swans looked in. And because it was on a bend of the river, you looked towards the Tower and Tower Bridge with the dome of St Paul's behind them, to the left, and the docks to the right.'

Contrary to popular belief, Princess Margaret was not a regular visitor from the outset. 'I went most often after Tony and I were married,' she says. Nevertheless Rotherhithe Street did provide the setting for many enjoyable evenings: lively parties that went on into the small hours, quiet dinner parties with a few carefully chosen friends, or simply relaxing à deux. On occasions such as these Tony would prepare simple meals and the Princess would wash the dishes afterwards in the small sink.

Another royal visitor who enjoyed the room's relaxed ambience was Queen Elizabeth the Queen Mother. Late one evening, when the streets were deserted, she joined the Princess and Tony on one of their post-wedding trips to Rotherhithe Street. En route they stopped to take a leisurely walk along Waterloo Road, pausing now and then to look in shop windows, including that of a well-known tattooist. For the Queen Mother in particular it was the first chance she had had of taking an unhurried look at an area she had only ever known as an official royal visitor.

Remarkably, no word linking Princess Margaret's name with

Armstrong-Jones was ever leaked to the press throughout the entire period which led to the announcement of their engagement – or perhaps it is more accurate to say that no leaks were ever taken seriously. Tony's professional association with the Royal Family, not to mention his well-known liaison with the Chinese actress Jacqui Chan, who had appeared in *Kismet*, *The Teahouse of the August Moon* and *The World of Suzie Wong*, provided the most effective of covers. Furthermore, when the couple went out together in public, it was almost invariably as part of a group of friends.

The lack of curiosity about Armstrong-Jones may have been due to a number of reasons, but probably to two in particular. Firstly, since the end of the Townsend affair, it had been widely assumed that no man was likely to become a permanent fixture in Princess Margaret's life, and secondly, a photographer, no matter how personable, hardly seemed an acceptable candidate for the Princess's hand. It is not surprising, therefore, that Princess Margaret and Armstrong-Jones were able to act fairly normally, without arousing the suspicions of Fleet Street gossip-mongers. Together they entertained their friends at Rotherhithe Street and at Clarence House, but were careful not to accept or encourage return invitations lest they should be discovered.

In the early summer of 1959 a series of official photographs of Princess Margaret was taken to mark her twenty-ninth birthday. The photographer was, of course, Tony. Meeting Cecil Beaton not long afterwards at a show of silk designs that Oliver Messel, Graham Sutherland and he had organized, the Princess confessed, 'I've been faithless to you.'

'I knew at once that she meant that she had had her photograph taken by T.A.J.', Beaton noted in his diary. 'This was a blow, but I thought it extremely honest and frank to tell me before the pictures appeared. I showed great tact by muttering, "I'm *so* glad. He's such a nice young man and deserves his success. If I have to have a rival, I'm glad it's him and not Baron."'

By the time the photographs appeared in August to a very favourable response, Tony had been invited by the Queen to stay at Balmoral. His deepening friendship with Princess Margaret added to the air of excitement on Deeside. The Queen – then thirty-three – was expecting her third baby the following February (an historic event since no child had been born to a reigning sovereign since the

days of Queen Victoria), and although Princess Margaret did not
have marriage on her mind just yet, her mother and sister undoubtedly did.

A few weeks later, just before the Royal Family returned to
London, matters took an unexpected turn, to Tony's ultimate benefit. Princess Margaret received a letter from Brussels in which Peter
Townsend broke the news that he was to remarry: he had fallen in
love with a nineteen-year-old girl called Marie-Luce Jamagne. To
the Princess it came as a bolt from the blue, not only because it was
the last thing she had expected but also because it was a betrayal of
an understanding they had reached 'concerning remarriage after
divorce'.

That October afternoon, while they were out walking, Princess
Margaret told Armstrong-Jones of Townsend's revelation. But in
anticipation of what seemed inevitable, she told Tony not to ask her
to marry him. 'He eventually did, but in a roundabout way. It was
very cleverly worded,' she recalls.

Two months later, in December 1959, the Princess and Tony
became privately engaged and, although she is alleged to have
remarked that her acceptance, coming as it did at the time of
Townsend's second marriage, was 'no coincidence', the Princess
strongly denies that she was marrying on the rebound.

'I'm *so* pleased you are going to marry Margaret,' the Queen
Mother, in ebullient mood, told Tony.

'Sssh,' he replied, 'I haven't asked the Queen yet.'

His opportunity to do so came one month later while the Royal
Family was staying at Sandringham. Yet even then a watertight
excuse was needed to explain Tony's presence. It was provided by, of
all things, a statue: in the garden of Sandringham House sat a Buddha
known to the Royal Family as 'John Chinaman', which had originally been screened by a wooden fretwork pergola that had long since
perished. On the pretext of presenting a design for a new pergola,
Armstrong-Jones arrived at the house one January morning in 1960,
bringing with him a perfect scale model.

The Queen greeted him and a little later retired to her room to
work for an hour or two. Then at last she rang for her Page: 'Ask
Mr Armstrong-Jones to bring in his model.' Behind closed doors
Tony formally asked Her Majesty's permission to marry Princess
Margaret. Permission was granted and the Princess, together with

the Queen Mother and Prince Philip were called in – still ostensibly to approve the Buddha's pergola. That something which seemed so insignificant could cause sounds of such jubilation from the adjoining room must have been a source of surprise to the rest of the Royal Family's guests, the more so since the screen was not mentioned again and not so much as another glance was cast towards Tony's model.

The impending royal birth and Princess Margaret's wish that news of her engagement should not eclipse the event meant that the betrothal announcement was to be withheld for the time being. At the end of January the Royal Family returned to London and at Buckingham Palace on 19 February 1960 Her Majesty gave birth to her second son, Prince Andrew. Precisely one week later, during the early evening of Friday 26 February, the following announcement was made from Clarence House:

> It is with the greatest pleasure that Queen Elizabeth the Queen Mother announces the betrothal of her beloved daughter The Princess Margaret to Mr Antony Charles Robert Armstrong-Jones, son of Mr R. O. L. Armstrong-Jones Q.C., and the Countess of Rosse, to which union The Queen has gladly given her consent.

The following month, the *London Gazette*, foremost chronicler of such events, officially recorded the Queen's pleasure at the forthcoming marriage:

> At the Court at Buckingham Palace, the 16th day of March, 1960. Present, The Queen's Most Excellent Majesty, Lord Chancellor, Lord President, Mr Secretary Butler, Sir Michael Adeane, Chancellor of the Duchy of Lancaster. Her Majesty was pleased this day, in pursuance of the Royal Marriages Act 1772, to declare Her Consent to a Contract of Matrimony between Her Sister Her Royal Highness The Princess Margaret Rose and Antony Charles Robert Armstrong-Jones Esquire, which Consent Her Majesty has caused to be signified under the Great Seal and to be entered in the Books of the Privy Council.

Public reaction to the engagement was one of undisguised astonishment and delight.

In its leader *The Times* enthused vigorously:

> The announcement of Princess Margaret's engagement to marry will be enthusiastically welcomed throughout the Commonwealth on the simple assurance that Her Royal Highness is following her own heart,

and that the Queen is delighted with her choice. The Princess, who has a keen sense of humour and a justifiable distaste for impertinent prying into her private life, will perhaps derive a little extra pleasure from the thought that, after so much confident speculation about her probable intentions, she has eventually sprung a complete surprise.

Elsewhere, the reaction was decidedly less ecstatic. 'Lunched with the Duchess [of Kent, otherwise Princess Marina] and Princess Alexandra. They are *not* pleased over Princess Margaret's engagement. There was a distinct *froideur* when I mentioned it', noted Noël Coward. Disapproval was not so surprising from Princess Marina, however, for she always held very definite – not to say very grand – ideas about the calibre of person a member of the Royal Family should be permitted to marry. Nor was it particularly surprising to learn that many of Tony's own circle, as well as his father, were very much against the proposed marriage; indeed the unanimous feeling was that the Princess and her fiancé were too much alike in temperament and too different in background for the marriage to be happy – once their love became commonplace, as it was bound to do, they would never cease to be at loggerheads. Tony could never properly belong to the Royal Family, his temperament would never allow it, and Princess Margaret, try as she might to adapt to Tony's way of life, could never be anything but a part of the Royal Family. It was the only world she knew.

A stupefied Jocelyn Stevens, who had known Tony since their Eton days, says he urged him to have an affair with the Princess, but strongly advised against marriage. Upset though Tony was by the lack of enthusiasm amongst his friends, he still ensured that each of them received an invitation to the wedding.

While preparations for the marriage were in progress, for his protection Armstrong-Jones moved out of 20 Pimlico Road and into Buckingham Palace at the Queen's invitation. And it was from there on 1 March that he drove the short distance to Clarence House to dine with the Queen Mother and Princess Margaret. Later that same evening, he and the Princess officially appeared in public together for the first time, when they accompanied Queen Elizabeth to a gala ballet performance at the Royal Opera House. Outside in Bow Street a vast crowd had gathered to catch a glimpse of the newly engaged couple, while inside, as they entered the royal box, the audience of more than two thousand gave them a standing ovation. That night Princess Margaret was dressed in a strapless evening gown of embroidered satin and wore as a necklace the main supports of the spectacular diamond tiara she was to wear at her wedding.

Of the Princess's engagement ring, a ruby set at the centre of a series of diamond leaves, some journalists openly asserted that it had belonged to Tony's mother. Overlooking the immense professional success he enjoyed, they claimed that he could not possibly have bought it. Denials were made, but it was not until the Countess of Rosse produced her own ruby ring that the stories were finally quashed. Lady Rosse eventually gave this ring to her granddaughter, Lady Sarah Armstrong-Jones, as a christening present.

Not long after the engagement was announced, Princess Margaret and Tony Armstrong-Jones drove south to Bath to spend a weekend at the home of close friends of Tony, Jeremy Fry and his wife. Invited over from his house at Broadchalke for Sunday lunch, Cecil Beaton noted in his diary:

I set off in high excitement and good deal of anxiety at the difficulty of finding the way. Crowds outside the house – policemen, journalists, bumpkins. The door was opened by T.A.J. and Jeremy Fry and we stood talking in a most informal atmosphere in the hall that was hung with the most modern of pictures. In the next room a babble of voices and more violent pictures; and young men with long hair and jeans, young women with equally long hair and sweaters – an artistic group, all very unpretentious and most sympathetic. Tony, very blue-eyed and alert, was full of quiet excitement and vitality. In the midst of this milling party group, looking very simple and homey, was the bride-to-be. Her complexion was exquisitely pink and white and her hair was chic enough to differentiate her from the others.

I made a speech to Princess Margaret saying that I thought she had found the most delightful solution for me as to how, most charmingly, to get rid of a rival photographer. She roared with laughter and asked me to repeat the sentence to Tony. But I bungled it ... Then I was shown the first communal wedding present. One of the painters present had given them a large picture of a great number of hysterical-looking naked figures milling together in what appeared to be a blue haze or an earthquake or a trench scene of the 1914–18 war. Princess Margaret said, 'They're all dancing.' I took a gulp of champagne and said, 'Oh, I'm so glad it isn't a disaster.' Princess Margaret laughed so much that she had to lie flat in an armchair.

The lunch that followed was simple and delightful. Food the usual English Sunday fare – beef, with uncooked carrots, heavy apple tart – and Tony helping round with the vegetables. Coffee drunk from mugs without saucers. Tony's piercing eyes occasionally transfixed on his affianced one, in a trance of love. In an undertone he would call her 'my pet'. She seemed like a ripe peach, all bloom and rosiness.

The house was under siege from the Press. Tony confided – 'We're hemmed in here – we'd like to go for a walk and get some air – could we come over to you this afternoon? Otherwise we don't know where to go.' I was delighted … The party toured the garden – which was looking very wintry with only a few signs of spring; then the lovers went off for a walk – Tony in his shirt sleeves doing a Sir Walter Raleigh act as Princess Margaret got over the barbed wire fences to climb to the downs.

During the next few weeks a spate of announcements concerning the arrangements for the royal wedding was released from the press office at Clarence House. After much consultation and checking of official diaries within the Royal Family, Friday 6 May was settled upon as the most convenient date for the ceremony, though the Princess received innumerable letters from superstitious members of the public. They reminded her that it was held unlucky to be married on a Friday and, of course, quoted the rhyme concerning the month: 'Marry in May and rue the day.'

In addition to acknowledging the congratulatory messages received from all over the world in their tens of thousands, such letters also required replies. Nobody concerned could doubt that the tasks to be tackled in less than three months were enormous.

The marriage ceremony was to take place in Westminster Abbey, where the marriages of the Queen and the Queen Mother had been celebrated. If there were any doubts about a member of the Royal Family marrying a commoner in such a traditional royal setting, it was always possible to call on the precedent set by Queen Victoria's granddaughter Princess Patricia of Connaught (Lady Patricia Ramsay) in 1919, when she too married a commoner in Westminster Abbey.

The Princess and Armstrong-Jones met several times with Dr Eric Abbott, then Dean of Westminster, to plan the more personal details of the ceremony. For the most part, Princess Margaret selected the music, the hymns and the prayers that were to be part of the service. Her choice of music included works by Bach, Handel, Purcell, William Harris, Schubert, Gibbons and Holst, and instead of an Address, it was decided that the Beatitudes would be read.

On 24 March, it was announced that the Queen had placed the royal yacht *Britannia* at her sister's disposal for her honeymoon. One week later, with the ceremonial aspect of the wedding already well in hand, a statement from Clarence House announced that the bride, who was to be given away by her brother-in-law, the Duke of Edinburgh, would 'travel in the Glass Coach ... with a Captain's Escort of the Household Cavalry'. The route to be taken, though relatively short, followed a well-trodden path: the carriage procession would move down the Mall, across Horse Guards Parade into Whitehall, thence to Parliament Street and round the east and south sides of Parliament Square to the West Door of Westminster Abbey. The statement added, 'Princess Margaret and Mr Armstrong-Jones will return in the Glass Coach along the same route and back to Buckingham Palace.'

The Princess's eight child bridesmaids, chosen from the couple's families and friends were to be the bride's niece, Princess Anne, her first god-daughter Marilyn Wills (daughter of her cousin Jean), Tony's niece Catherine Vesey, Angela Nevill (daughter of the Royal Family's friends Lord and Lady Rupert Nevill), Virginia Fitzroy (daughter of the present Duke and Duchess of Grafton), Annabel Rhodes, Rose Nevill and Sarah Lowther. Roger Gilliatt, Professor of Clinical Neurology at London University, proved the ultimate choice for Best Man (or Groomsman as he is known in royal circles); Cecil Beaton was commissioned to take the official photographs and Norman Hartnell, who had dressed the Queen, the Queen Mother and Princess Margaret for a number of years, was asked to design the dresses for all three on this occasion.

Hartnell's brief for Princess Margaret's bridal gown could not have been much clearer, for, although it was not publicized at all, dressing his bride allowed Armstrong-Jones's own ideas on fashion to be utilized. For maximum effect, he stipulated that both the dress and veil were to be severely plain in order to act as a foil to the Princess's head-dress. Her hair was to be done in a simple *chignon* around which would be set a magnificent diadem, several inches deep and worked completely in diamonds. Known as the Poltimore

Tiara, it had been privately acquired at auction, for a rumoured £5,000, specifically for Princess Margaret.

Hartnell, renowned throughout his career for his love of heavily embroidered dresses for his royal clients, produced for Princess Margaret a wedding dress that both astounded and delighted the fashion world. There was not so much as a solitary sequin, pearl, bead or crystal to be seen on it anywhere. It was, as the bridegroom had instructed, severely plain. 'It made its effect not with glitter, but with an art that conceals art' said *Country Life*. Worn over stiffened tulle underskirts, the dress was made from thirty yards of white silk organza. It had a fitted V-neck bodice with wrist-length sleeves and a full, almost crinoline skirt of twelve panels, which formed a semicircular train several feet long. The bridal veil, created to Hartnell's design by Claude St Cyr of Paris, was made from the finest silk organza and was edged with the same piping as the dress.

By noon on Friday 6 May, the temperature had risen to 72°F and all London was *en fête*. The Mall was hung with white silk banners emblazoned with Tudor roses bearing the couple's entwined initials, while a sixty-foot 'triumphal' arch garlanded with real and artificial roses spanned the junction of the Mall and Stable Yard Road outside Clarence House. Government buildings along Whitehall were bright with white hydrangeas and stocks arranged around red roses, and Parliament Square was a profusion of spring flowers. Twelve masts, from which were suspended garlands and enormous baskets of pink hydrangeas and yellow marguerites, added to the festive air, while flower-beds were a blaze of colour from masses of red, gold and orange tulips, and in raised *jardinières* were great displays of wisteria, rhododendrons and laburnums. Never before had London seen such a spectacular array of street decorations for a royal wedding. Indeed, it was arguably the most appealing occasion of its kind to date.

Of the 2,068 guests who were seated inside Westminster Abbey, only about eight hundred of them had a guaranteed chance of seeing anything of the processions or even of the wedding ceremony itself except on the television monitors which had been positioned for the guests' benefit along the nave. Theirs was the honour and privilege of a seat inside; for those outside – a crowd estimated at half a million – finding standing room was a challenge made worthwhile for the thrill of a glimpse of the royal coach. Many people had begun to assemble as much as a week before; 'being there' was, for them, far preferable to watching the ceremony on television, as millions throughout the country were doing. This was the first royal wedding to be transmitted 'live' on television, an innovation which greatly appealed to the Princess herself: 'It meant that those of my friends who couldn't come could still see it. I loved that idea.'

Princess Margaret arrived at Westminster Abbey early, due to Prince Philip's warnings that if she did not hurry herself, they were certainly going to be late. Once the bride had stepped down from the Glass Coach beneath the awning at the West Door of the Abbey, footmen assisting with her voluminous train, a fanfare, composed by Sir Arthur Bliss, Master of The Queen's Musick, was sounded by the Kneller Hall Trumpeters and the great organ boomed to life as the choir, supplemented by the men and boys of Her Majesty's Chapels Royal, prepared to sing the processional hymn, 'Christ is made the sure Foundation'. So began the long, four-minute walk up the blue-carpeted nave to the steps of the sacrarium. Behind the bride walked her young attendants, each carrying a small posy of lilies-of-the-valley and wearing copies of a white organza dress threaded with blue ribbon that had been particularly liked by George VI when his daughter had worn it in the past. Of all the decisions Princess Margaret had taken in connexion with her wedding, this was undoubtedly the most personal.

As the bride's procession moved momentarily out of view – passing through the arch of the ornate Choir Screen, designed by Edward Blore more than a century earlier – Prince Philip struck a lighter note amidst all the solemnity by asking the Princess:

'Am I holding on to you, or are you holding on to me?'

'I'm holding on to you,' Princess Margaret replied.

'I don't know who's more nervous,' said the Prince, 'you or me.'

At the foot of the sacrarium steps, the bride turned and handed her bouquet of orchids to Princess Anne. The Dean of Westminster stood before the couple and opened the marriage service, reading from the 1928 Prayer Book, and minutes later, the Archbishop of Canterbury stepped forward to conduct the rest of the ceremony from the 1662 version.

In the exchange of vows, the responses of both the bride and bridegroom were clearly heard and at one point, instead of speaking after the Archbishop of Canterbury, Princess Margaret jumped ahead of him. 'I knew the words so well,' she explains. 'I'd practised them over and over, so that instead of repeating "From this day forward" I beat the Archbishop to the next line, "For better, for worse".'

At the end of the ceremony the bride and bridegroom made their way to the Chapel of St Edward the Confessor and there with members of their families they signed the marriage registers. During this short interval the choir sang two anthems: 'I will not leave you comfortless, Alleluia' by William Byrd and 'Lord, who hast made us for thine own' by Holst. Then a final fanfare rang out. The Princess and her husband appeared in the chapel doorway to the side of the High Altar and, to Purcell's 'Trumpet Tune and Airs', they crossed the sacrarium, pausing to honour the Queen and the Queen Mother, who had by now returned to their seats.

As the couple re-entered the nave, the bridesmaids curtsied to Princess Margaret and followed her through the congregation and out to the response of the vast crowds. In Dean's Yard the Glass Coach was drawn up and the bridegroom climbed in first to assist the Princess. Once she was settled, the procession with its escort of the Household Cavalry moved off into Broad Sanctuary and rode to Buckingham Palace for the wedding breakfast.

When the crowd was finally allowed to move forward, led by a police cordon – through which many broke to run to the palace railings – the cry went up 'We want Margaret!' They were rewarded as the balcony doors were opened and the bride and bridegroom, together with their attendants and families stepped out.

Later that afternoon Princess Margaret and her husband left Buckingham Palace in an open-topped Rolls-Royce to drive through the City of London to join the royal yacht *Britannia*. In the narrow City streets, the royal car was often slowed to walking pace as people left their offices to cheer the progress of the bridal couple. Buttons scratched the car's maroon paintwork as it edged forward and city policemen fought in vain to keep the crowds on the pavements.

Twenty minutes late, Princess Margaret and her husband finally arrived at Battle Bridge Pier to a salute of ships' sirens, pealing church bells and the acclaim of thousands lining the river banks on either side of the Pool of London.

Britannia herself was dressed overall and as the Princess and Armstrong-Jones stepped from the royal barge to board the yacht by the starboard after gangway – in keeping with royal tradition – the flags disappeared through the trapdoor in the funnel. As they did so, Princess Margaret's personal standard (which is the royal Coat-of-Arms 'differenced' by a white bar or 'label of three points argent') was raised to the top of the main mast. Five minutes later, the royal yacht slipped anchor and, with the band of the Royal Marines playing 'Oh, What a Beautiful Morning', began to move slowly downstream.

At 5.40 p.m. *Britannia* passed between the raised bascules of Tower Bridge, and from the yacht's bridge the Princess and Armstrong-Jones acknowledged the cheers of the crowds. One person who received a special wave from the couple was William Glenton. By now returned from Westminster Abbey, he leant from his window above the 'white room' at 59 Rotherhithe Street to watch *Britannia*'s impressive departure.

As the general feeling of euphoria began to simmer down and some MPs inevitably started to moan about the cost of the wedding, which was said to have been in the region of £25,000, the royal yacht headed towards the Caribbean, where Princess Margaret and her husband had chosen to spend their honeymoon. It was while they were on this six-week cruise of the islands that Princess Margaret took her first look at a much smaller, and then unknown, island on which a modest house would eventually be built for her – partly to make up for the lack of her own country retreat at home.

Mustique in the Windward Islands, which contained 1,250 un-developed acres, eight beaches and two harbours, is three miles long and one mile wide. It had recently been bought by the Princess's enterprising friend, Lord Glenconner. 'When I knew Princess Margaret was getting married,' he says, 'I asked her if she would like a present in a box or a plot of land on Mustique. She chose the land.'

The Princess and her husband first set foot on the island's white sands on 26 May 1960 and, at that time, the precise location of Tennant's wedding-gift was undecided. To Tony Armstrong-Jones its situation would ever remain a mystery. He never went to the island again.

On 18 June, the royal yacht – its decks lined by officers and ratings of the ship's company – sailed into Portsmouth Harbour at the end of her voyage. Shortly afterwards a formally dressed Princess Margaret and Tony Armstrong-Jones – she in pink silk, he in a grey lounge suit – stepped ashore, acknowledging the greetings of the crowd waiting to see them.

The question of a home had, of course, already been settled, at least temporarily. Number 10 Kensington Palace was, by royal standards, small. Tucked away to the side of the visitors' entrance to the palace's state apartments, it had for many years been the home of a distant relation, the Marquess of Carisbrooke, a grandson of Queen Victoria, known within the Royal Family as 'Cousin Drino'. At his death in February 1960, the Queen, who was anxious for her sister to have a house of her own, seized the opportunity of ear-marking it before it was reallocated as a grace-and-favour residence.

Alterations to number 10 were kept to the bare minimum because its inconvenient size made any idea of long-term occupation unsuitable. For minor royal figures, the house would have been ideal, but for a senior-ranking Princess, expected to be responsible for her share of official entertaining, the modest proportions of the drawing-room and the even smaller dining-room meant that it was acceptable only as a temporary measure.

Now that the couple were home, Tony Armstrong-Jones began to taste the reality of what being absorbed into the Royal Family meant. Walking the prescribed one pace behind his royal wife, he started to accompany Princess Margaret on her official engagements. Their first, an afternoon performance of the Royal Tournament at Earls Court, took place ten days after their return from honeymoon. Regarded as a public figure in his own right, Tony found that it was not long before he was expected to perform the occasional solo engagement. The first, that December, took him to Newcastle where, appropriately, he presented prizes to the winners of the 1960 National Photographic Competition. An engagement which at first appeared rather less appropriate took place some months later when he opened the Congress of the International Union of Architects, and addressed the 1,500 delegates at the Royal Festival Hall. For a man who – according to his friends – 'didn't want to owe anything to anybody', his acceptance of this invitation may have looked like a sudden change of mind. Tony had indeed been uneasy about it, realizing that had he not been Princess Margaret's husband the invitation would not have been extended.

'Tony and I talked it over, and I said that I thought it was a very good idea,' the Princess says, recalling her husband's indecision. 'I told him that if he had views on architecture that he wanted to put forward, then he should do so.'

For the Princess and her husband the end of 1960 and the start of 1961 found them busy with all manner of public duties, including specific requests from the Queen. Her first was that they officially represent her at the wedding in Brussels of the Belgian King Baudouin to Dona Fabiola de Mora y Aragon, which was to take place shortly before Christmas, and a month later, after they had seen in the New Year with Tony's family in County Offaly, that they again represent her at the marriage in Oslo of Princess Astrid of Norway and Mr Johan Ferner.

There were the inevitable charity balls and gala performances to attend and, during the spring, visits to a new council development in Dumbartonshire, to the Wedgwood pottery at Darlaston, near Stoke-on-Trent, to the service of consecration at Guildford Cathedral, to Crediton in Devon, to York for a St John's Ambulance Rally (at which the Princess, as Commandant-in-Chief, was dressed in her black, bemedalled uniform and cockaded tricorn hat), and to the annual Chelsea Flower Show, when the couple were accompanied by Tony's mother and stepfather, Lord and Lady Rosse.

Once firmly settled in 10 Kensington Palace, Princess Margaret was rather surprised to find that Tony's thoughts were gravitating towards parenthood. It was a subject they had not previously discussed. In fact, one intimate friend of the couple remains firmly convinced, even now, that they rarely discussed anything of importance directly related to themselves. Her husband's desire for children was, however, realized and, on 25 May 1961, as she visited the Royal National Nose, Ear and Throat Hospital in London, the news that Princess Margaret was expecting her first baby that November was released.

During the first few months of his marriage to the Princess, it seemed to some that Tony was already showing signs of becoming restless with his limited role of action as his wife's consort. Together, on a personal level, however, few couples are likely to find such complete happiness. The Princess, never more attractive and at peace with herself, exuded a magnetism which her husband complemented perfectly. Friends have likened the reaction between them – the way in which each supported, encouraged and aided the other – to an electric current. Never the less, Tony needed something more.

Indeed it soon became clear that his decision to give up his career as a photographer in 1959 was making him frustrated and unhappy. Jocelyn Stevens says, 'It was like a pilot sacrificing his career for his marriage ... but watching every 'plane with the thought, "I should be up there".'

A joke advertisement which had appeared in a Sunday newspaper while the Princess and her husband were away on their honeymoon now had about it a pointed irony: 'Cambridge Blue, 29, well connected, forced to give up lucrative professional career, seeks release from social round. Own car. Suggestions welcomed.'

Suggestions were most certainly welcomed, as the question, 'What could Tony do?' was asked. In some respects Princess Margaret's marriage was an experiment. In general terms, the nation and even the Crown were witnessing something for which there was no precedent. Although Princess Patricia of Connaught had married Captain Alexander Ramsay, whose career had been at sea, she had relinquished her royal rank to take the courtesy title 'Lady', and her husband thus had little but his bachelor status to sacrifice on the great royal altar. Moreover, the positions of Princess Margaret and Lady Patricia in the royal hierarchy could not be compared.

A partial answer to Tony's problem was found in early 1961 when he joined the Council for Industrial Design, which later became the Design Council. Tony was to advise on various aspects of the Council's work promoting high standards amongst British designers. A statement issued by the Council, explained that 'the idea that Mr Armstrong-Jones should take an active part in the work of the Council was his own and arises out of his own personal interest in matters of architecture and design'. At his own request he received no fee or salary, but was provided with an office of his own near the Haymarket.

Fleet Street was outraged. It was a 'sinecure' the press thundered indignantly. But a sinecure without remuneration? How was that? The barrage he faced became even louder when London Zoo announced that it had chosen a design by Tony in conjunction with architect Cedric Price and consultant engineer Frank Newby for a new aviary. 'Tony's Birdcage' the press sneered, while one journalist was of the opinion that Armstrong-Jones ought to be classed as one of Britain's leading birdcage designers: 'not an overcrowded profession'.

It is a curious human sport that public figures like Princess

Margaret and Antony Armstrong-Jones should be elaborately positioned on pedestals only, it sometimes appears, for the enjoyment of
knocking them down. The couple had not been married long before
one of their critics, in mild vein, was writing: 'Her Royal Highness
the Princess Margaret and her husband, have provided the country
with more interest, amusement, amazement and stupefaction than
any royal personages since Prinnie [sic] and Mrs Fitzherbert'.

The expected birth of Princess Margaret's first baby began renewed
speculation about a title for its father. The argument had already
been given one airing at the time of the couple's marriage. On 5
May 1960, the day after the grand, pre-wedding ball at Buckingham
Palace, the headline of the *Daily Mirror* had declared: 'A Title for
Tony? What NONSENSE!' The newspaper's 'Page One Comment'
went on:

> Earl This ... or Viscount That ... or The Duke of Heaven-knows-
> What. What nonsense it is! Does young Tony want a title? No. Does he
> deserve a Title? No. Maybe he will deserve a title later on. Maybe we
> all will. But on what possible grounds does he rate a title now? Mr Jones
> fell in love with a princess and a princess fell in love with him. All good
> luck to HRH Princess Margaret and happiness to the gay young couple.
> But Lord Antony? Viscount Armstrong? Earl Jones? Oh no, please no!'

The question of a peerage for Tony had in fact already been
discussed at the Palace. Although the Queen had never considered
offering him more than an earldom – of where was to be a matter
for the couple to decide – wild stories flew around, all without a
grain of truth, that Princess Margaret had set her heart on a dukedom
for her husband. If her sister's husband could be created a duke,
claimed one story, then the Princess wanted the same honour for
Tony. Defending herself vigorously on that point, she exclaims, 'I
know my place!'

With his elevation more or less within sight, Princess Margaret
decided against adding the suffix 'Mrs Antony Armstrong-Jones' to
her title because, 'I imagined I would be thought a snob for taking
a double-barrelled name. But the press shortened it anyway and
called me "Mrs Jones" ... I got so tired of it in the end.' Tony's
peerage was, however, finally to alter that.

After giving the matter lengthy consideration, Tony finally decided to be known as the first Earl of Snowdon, Viscount Linley of Nymans. The public announcement to that effect was made on 3 October 1961, but, as may have been anticipated, to disgruntled noises. Closer to home the reaction was one of pleasure. 'I think it's splendid,' said Tony's former stepmother, Carol Coombe. 'I just love the title ... I'm about to send a telegram off to the dear boy.'

Precisely one month later, on Friday 3 November, another official communiqué announced: 'Her Royal Highness The Princess Margaret, Countess of Snowdon, was safely delivered of a son at 10.45 a.m. today'; and the new Earl told waiting journalists, 'The Princess and I are absolutely thrilled and delighted.'

The baby, who automatically assumed his father's subsidiary title of Viscount Linley, weighed 6lb 4oz at birth and six weeks later he was christened David Albert Charles in the Music Room at Buckingham Palace.

CHAPTER TEN

THE SNOWDONS

The Snowdons, as Princess Margaret and her husband became known, were widely regarded in Britain during the 'swinging sixties' as *the* most glamorous couple. In the game of social one-up-manship, to know them was considered by many the supreme accolade. Dubbed by Beatle John Lennon with good-natured irreverence as 'Priceless Margarine and Bony Armstrove', they were the subject of frequent discussion and found their every move worthy of press attention. If almost everything the Princess did before her marriage seemed to find its way into print, the volume of press items was now even greater.

A teenager was able to make immediate news when, in February 1961, he stole Princess Margaret's black convertible and took it on a joy-ride while the Princess and Tony were lunching with friends. Press photographers lurked constantly in the background to catch the Princess in her off-duty moments. One resulting picture showed her standing in the Old Parade Ground at Kensington Palace – now a wide, grassy enclosure – watching the Russian astronaut Yuri Gagarin drive to the Soviet Embassy, and another photograph captured her in a satin maternity dress shortly before the birth of her son as she was leaving the Queen's Theatre in Shaftesbury Avenue after seeing *Stop the World – I Want to Get Off*.

Of more immediate concern than press attention, however, was the question of Lord Snowdon's own career. His involvement with the activities of the Design Council had pushed the subject into the background temporarily, but it was increasingly clear that he needed the professional creative outlet that photography had provided for him in the past. The first question about his proposed return to work was whether there would be any objections from his royal in-laws, but here he was met by the combined forces of the Queen and Princess Margaret who both urged him to pick up the threads of his career. There was, they reasoned, nothing to stop him. Given their assurances, a further question remained: precisely who would offer him a job on his own merits, regardless of whether this might appear to be currying favour with the Royal Family?

It has been generally accepted that Mark Boxer, a friend of Snowdon's since the early 1950s and at this time working on the *Sunday Times* magazine, was responsible for providing a solution, but there was, in fact, rather more to it than that. Princess Margaret, anxious about her husband's frustrations and resolved to help, called upon the confidential services of Jocelyn Stevens, who was asked to make it known to Denis Hamilton, editor of the *Sunday Times*, that should a suitable job for her husband be available, Lord Snowdon would be pleased to accept. Hamilton had not, of course, previously considered such a possibility, but there was, he said, no question that Tony would be an asset to the newspaper's embryonic Sunday magazine and a position on the staff would be justified by his talents, not because he was the Queen's brother-in-law.

News of Tony's appointment to the *Sunday Times* – as Artistic Adviser, a post that would involve a considerable amount of travelling on photographic assignments – was released in January 1962 to an immediate, though not wholly unexpected, backlash. Roy (later Lord) Thomson, the owner of the newspaper, defended the appointment when asked outright why Snowdon and not some other out-of-work photojournalist was being given the job. 'Because I don't know of a better unemployed photojournalist,' came his candid reply.

Yet if Lord Snowdon was unable to conceal his delight, David Astor, editor of the *Observer*, found it difficult to conceal his disgust. 'Mr Thomson', he said, 'carefully avoids the main issue, which is whether linking his expansionist aims to the Queen's family is likely to be good for the monarchy.' And on television, Mr Astor reasserted his claim that making use of the monarchy's 'fame' to 'put money into the pockets of a private firm' was not only a 'doubtful procedure' but potentially harmful to the standing of the monarchy. It was difficult to see how this could be, and now, from a safe distance, David Astor's objections look to have been based as much on patriotic concern for the welfare of the monarchy as on professional jealousy.

However, it could not be overlooked that until 1959 Antony Armstrong-Jones had been a businessman, and on the premise that professional outsiders posed a threat to the Crown, the whole issue might have been reignited the following year when the Hon. Angus Ogilvy – who held more than fifty City directorships – married the Queen's first cousin, Alexandra of Kent.

That the possibility of his giving up his business interests at the time of his marriage was never seriously considered indicated that a hurdle in the history of the Royal Family had been cleared. Lord Snowdon's appointment had been a 'first' in that history and it was clear that in future there would be little objection to the husband of a Princess pursuing an independent career.

Throughout 1961 another matter was uppermost in the minds of Princess Margaret and Lord Snowdon: a new and permanent home. Apartment 1A Clock Court, Kensington Palace, hidden from public view and well out of bounds to tourists, adjoins the south front of what the seventeenth-century diarist John Evelyn called 'a very sweete villa'. The house, comprising twenty-one rooms including the staff quarters, occupies one complete wing of Clock Court, originally designed for William and Mary by Sir Christopher Wren as the carriage approach to the state entrance, although it is no longer used as such.

On four storeys, the house forms the vertical and largest portion of what was originally apartment number one. The conversion of the T-shaped wing into two separate residences occurred in the middle of the present century when it was offered in its entirety to the widowed Duchess of Kent, Princess Marina, who found it was far too big for her needs. The Ministry of Works was called in and alterations made to provide a modernized apartment for Princess Marina, who lived there for the next twenty years.

However, the other part of the house was left untouched and the newly designated apartment 1A continued to stand empty, literally rotting from attic to basement and visited by none save the royal ghosts of its past. After William and Mary, the apartments were lived in by George I and George II, and became home to the extraordinary Princess Caroline of Brunswick, estranged wife of the

Prince Regent, afterwards George IV. Later still the Regent's brother, Augustus, Duke of Sussex, the sixth and most radical of George
III's nine sons, set up home here and, on the first floor, founded and
carefully maintained the famous Sussex Library.

Of Queen Victoria's nine children, two of her daughters, the
Princesses Louise and Beatrice, came to live at Kensington Palace,
and it was Princess Louise and her husband, the Marquess of Lorne,
afterwards Duke of Argyle, who were the last occupants of the
house before the Snowdons took it over. It remained Princess
Louise's official residence from the 1870s until 1939, the year in
which she died at the age of ninety-one.

Twenty-two years later, the sight which greeted Princess Margaret and Lord Snowdon warned them of the monumental task that
lay ahead. The entrance hall, running the length of the house, was
dark and unwelcoming, and from it was entered a vast, hall-like
room of daunting proportions. On the far side, five tall casement
windows, several feet apart, looked out on to a large, open garden
where once had stood a studio: Princess Louise was an accomplished
artist and sculptor. This 'hall' – last decorated in 1891 – had been the
drawing-room, which contemporary photographs in the possession
of Princess Margaret show full of furniture in the heaviest style of
the late Victorians. The walls were hung with gas lamps, innumerable paintings and family pictures, while unsightly strapping broke
the surface of the ceiling; all of which evoked an air of general
gloom.

Beyond the drawing-room lay another, smaller room, and on the
other side of a broad oak staircase, where the floor level unexpectedly
drops by several steps, was a garden room, once believed to have
been a guard-chamber. Here were three very large windows, one of
which had led into the garden until it had been bricked up at
Princess Louise's command; through it, she had discovered, her
husband stole for secret assignations with his lovers.

Apart from the need for total redecoration, the rampant decay,
'alive' walls of plaster, sand and kapock, and rotting floorboards
meant that Princess Margaret and her husband would have to gut
the house to make it habitable. A sum of £55,000 was allocated by
the Government for the work, although considerably more than
that amount was required. Indeed Princess Margaret had made it
clear that she did not want the Department of the Environment to

spend money on her behalf. The announcement of the Government's grant, however, was accompanied by outbursts of protest in the House of Commons. The Snowdons were once again at the centre of a controversy on which the news media were quick to capitalize. Princess Margaret, thundered certain MPs, was now in receipt of £15,000 a year from the Civil List and surely her husband expected handsome remuneration from his *Sunday Times* appointment.

The Princess's annuity has always provided ready ammunition for her critics to hurl on occasions such as this, and, however unjustified, the criticism now came as no surprise. What was overlooked was that the grant provided to assist in the work involved at 1A Clock Court was not merely to help provide a comfortable home for Princess Margaret and her family, but to help preserve a building of historic importance which is owned by the nation. Moreover, the Government's contribution towards the restoration of this Wren building was minimal compared to Government expenditure on other historic properties. Dyrham Park in Gloucestershire was a case in point. In 1957 this once magnificent seventeenth-century mansion was purchased by the Government for just over £5,000, then no small amount. A further £108,000 was subsequently spent on the property and by the time it was sold to the National Trust, later that year, total Government expenditure amounted to around £200,000.

The storm in a teacup over the Government grant was quickly over but it was only one of many attacks that were to be made by back-bench MPs on Princess Margaret during the 1960s and 1970s.

Much of the renovation at Kensington Palace, including structural work, was tackled personally by Lord Snowdon, who took pains to ensure that every penny of the Government grant was eked out in order to keep within the budget. Floors, ceilings, supports and walls were replaced. The entrance hall floor was repaved with black and white tiles of Welsh stone, the new walls were painted white, and the lattice-windows hung with long, olive-green curtains. The brick 'window' in the garden room was torn down and the casement restored. Today this is an especially pleasing room. The walls are drag-painted a warm rose-pink, and the off-white wall cabinets - almost floor-to-ceiling - house Princess Margaret's considerable collection of sea-shells, which experts from the Natural

The Princess aged
three (*Popperfoto*)

The Duke and
Duchess of York with
their daughters and
Allah at the circus,
1935 (*Central Press*)

Coronation Day of George VI and Queen Elizabeth, 12 May, 1937 (*Central Press*)

Princess Margaret representing the King for the first time at the Installation of Queen Juliana of the Netherlands with Princess Alice, Countess of Athlone (right), September 1948 (*Central Press*)

A formal twenty-first birthday photograph of Her Royal Highness by Cecil Beaton, 21 August, 1951 (*Central Press*)

Princess Margaret and her mother in the Irish State Coach en route to Westminster Abbey for the coronation of Queen Elizabeth II (*Central Press*)

Wedding group: (*standing left to right*) the Countess of Rosse, the Prince of Wales, the Queen, Antony Armstrong-Jones, Princess Margaret, Prince Philip, the Queen Mother and Ronald Armstrong-Jones, with the eight bridesmaids including Princess Anne (*third from right*) (*Cecil Beaton/Camera Press*)

Princess Margaret, Lord Snowdon and Viscount Linley leaving Kensington Palace for the christening of Lady Sarah Armstrong-Jones at Buckingham Palace in July 1964 (*Popperfoto*)

Princess Margaret talking to Richard Burton and Elizabeth Taylor at the 1967 Royal Film Performance of their film *The Taming of the Shrew*; Sir Michael Redgrave stands next to them, and Gina Lollobrigida looks on. The newspapers that day were full of stories about a rift between Princess Margaret and her husband (*Keystone*)

Princess Margaret and Lord Snowdon in the garden at Kensington Palace in 1967 (*Norman Parkinson/Camera Press*)

One of a series of portraits taken by Lord Snowdon in September 1967 to mark Princess Margaret's visit to Brussels for British Week (*Camera Press*)

In fancy-dress, Princess Margaret with Leonora Lichfield and Lord Glenconner at his fiftieth birthday party on Mustique in 1976 (*Camera Press*)

A military aircraft was turned into an ambulance to fly Princess Margaret to Sydney from Tuvala, where she had been taken seriously ill; she was greeted on arrival by the Governor, Sir Roden Cutler (*Keystone*)

Princess Margaret, wearing a mask designed by Carl Toms, leaves a charity ball accompanied by Norman Lonsdale. Behind them are (*left to right*) the Countess of Lichfield, lady-in-waiting the Hon. Annabel Whitehead, and Lady Anne Tennant (*Alan Davidson/Camera Press*)

History Museum have advised her is one of the finest in private ownership.

The major coup, however, was the transformation of Princess Louise's drawing-room, by far the largest and most impressive of the rooms on the ground floor. Set between the dining-room and what is now the library, previously Lord Snowdon's study, the present drawing-room successfully captures the style and mood of an eighteenth-century interior, which is precisely what Princess Margaret set out to do.

The simple colour combination of kingfisher-blue walls and pale grey curtains edged in blue and white sets off perfectly the main furnishings. The effect is of eighteenth-century elegance without being ostentatious – nor is the furnishing, as one journalist claimed, scaled down for the Princess's express comfort. 'I only wish it were,' she remarks.

Against the library wall stands a magnificent, six-panelled mahogany break-front cabinet housing a collection of porcelain, while nearby is a baby grand piano, given to the couple as a wedding present by the Earl and Countess of Rosse. Its lid is massed with family photographs – of Prince Charles and Princess Anne as children, of the Queen and Prince Philip after the coronation, of the Prince and Princess of Wales after their wedding and an especially appealing one of the Queen Mother who, as a joke, had draped a silk scarf over her tiara.

Armchairs and two sofas are arranged around the original fireplace, which was located by Lord Snowdon and has a surround of antique pine. The massive carpet in the room, designed by Carl Toms in subtle shades of blue, gold, apricot and grey, was also a wedding present, this time from the City of London.

At the far end of the room, beyond the writing table where Princess Margaret attends to all her desk work, a pair of prized blackamoor figures stand on either side of the double doors, veneered by the Snowdons themselves, that lead into the sand-coloured dining-room.

Visiting the house today, one is immediately aware of its 'lived in' atmosphere. It may be the official residence of a member of the Royal Family, but it is also Princess Margaret's home. It does not speak of untold luxury but rather of comfortable elegance, and with its large garden enclosed behind a high brick wall, the house could easily be taken for the quiet country residence William and Mary planned in their quest to escape the often fatal fogs of Westminster.

Five months after his elevation to the peerage, Lord Snowdon was formally introduced to the House of Lords. Following time-honoured tradition, and wearing a scarlet robe edged with ermine, he processed to the woolsack between his sponsors, the Earls of Leicester and Westmorland, preceded by The Earl Marshal, the Duke of Norfolk, and Sir Brian Horrocks, who held office as Black Rod. From the Commonwealth Gallery, Princess Margaret watched her husband as the formal ceremonial was observed; confirmation of the junior Earl's fealty was demanded and this he demonstrated by rising from his seat three times and doffing his tricorn hat in the direction of the throne.

In August, five months after the House of Lords ceremony, the Earl of Snowdon found himself sitting next to another throne, this time occupied by Princess Margaret, as she represented the Queen at ceremonies marking Jamaica's independence. It was the fourth time the Princess had visited Jamaica but only the first time she had officially represented the sovereign on the island. After Princess Margaret had taken the royal salute, she and her husband drove to Kingston and the King George VI Memorial Park. There the usual formal address of welcome was presented by the Mayor, before a Civic Welcome heralded the start of Her Royal Highness's mission.

The three-day visit culminated in a midnight ceremony on 5/6 August, when the Union Flag was slowly lowered, signifying the end of 307 years of British rule. Moments later, the new flag of independent Jamaica was raised on the floodlit mast. The following day, the Princess, dressed in white satin and wearing a diamond tiara, officially opened the island's first Parliament, in the formal setting of George William Gordon House, the Jamaican legislature.

If, as Jocelyn Stevens maintains, Lord Snowdon is fundamentally a shy, even reclusive man, he managed to cope with the rigours of formal royal tours and the frequent deadliness of official engagements without ever betraying his true feelings. Certainly to the world at large he and Princess Margaret were a sparkling gregarious couple, the mention of whose names alone spoke of a new kind of royalty. It could not be denied that, compared to them, the rest of the Royal Family was generally regarded as rather pedestrian, a group of people who by dint of royal office were interesting but who appeared to many to be anachronistic figures against a radically changing landscape.

The 1950s had already proved that, no matter how seriously Princess Margaret regarded the responsibilities of her position, she was also an individual. The decade that followed was, for her as for people generally, a time of relative freedom and new experiences. They were revolutionary years which not only suited Princess Margaret's temperament but which created a youthful 'movement' of which she and Tony were very much a part.

'I think music had a great influence on people in the sixties,' the Princess says today. And in that medium, the greatest phenomenon of all was, of course, the sound of the Beatles. 'I adored them', Princess Margaret recalls, 'because they were poets as well as musicians.'

Fashion also played a major part in expressing the new sense of freedom and the Princess found the changes in men's fashion particularly appealing. 'We both hated black-tie', she says, 'and when we invited friends to dinner, the men always asked what they should wear. We said anything but black-tie, and they always came in the most beautiful shirts.'

When women began raising their hemlines with the introduction of the mini-skirt, Princess Margaret's hemlines also rose a few inches. 'But I never wore mini-skirts which were very high,' she says, indicating mid-thigh. Nonetheless when the Princess took the salute at the 1982 Sovereign's Parade at Sandhurst, she was shown a photograph of herself as Reviewing Officer during the early 1970s and was amused to see the pleated skirt of her yellow suit cut to the requirements of fashion then. 'I can't believe that I actually looked like that!'

That Princess Margaret had married a man whose life was not governed by Society's 'seasons' meant that she became, to all intents and purposes, a part of a world that did what it wanted when it wanted. It was a world that had always beckoned to her: the bright lights of show business and the stimulating conversations of the literati. Whether she and Lord Snowdon were dining privately with the Irish writer Edna O'Brien, then living in Putney, singing duets in a Battersea restaurant, entertaining Margot Fonteyn and Rudolf Nureyev or the Goons, attending a private view or chatting in the Crush Bar of the Royal Opera House, Princess Margaret was in her element.

These were, of course, the early years when the Princess and Tony were still deeply engrossed in each other. They were times of tactile gestures, private asides, shared laughter and shared confidences. Days when the 'electric current' that friends spoke of provided glowing confirmation of inner emotions, and those who had warned them against marrying began to doubt the confidence with which they had predicted certain disaster.

The long-term success of the couple's marriage would never have been in doubt had the enchantment of those days remained with them. Indeed if the Princess and Lord Snowdon were aware of a 'formula' for the success of their relationship, it was that their feelings had been incubated in extraordinarily unreal circumstances. Although Princess Margaret affirms that they 'considered every consequence before getting engaged,' according to certain friends the couple's idea of marriage tended to resemble an extension of their days in what Cecil Beaton called 'Tony's slum'.

That Princess Margaret and her husband were seen by their circle – indeed by their families – as a 'dynamic' couple is a fact that cannot be stressed too often, because it illustrates the stark and bewildering contrast of what lay in store. But for now, at least, theirs was a marriage which soared above others, forging a colourful path along which the dazzled, excitable *papparazzi* followed.

On Sunninghill lake, near Windsor, the couple took up water-skiing with Jocelyn Stevens and his wife Jane (Sheffield), who was soon to become one of the Princess's extra ladies-in-waiting. It was a sport Princess Margaret enjoyed; clad in a skin-tight wet suit and a swimming cap, she would speed across the lake's surface, taking – along with the others – a frequent ducking into the bargain. Summer weekends were frequently spent in this way, with picnic lunches laid out at the water's edge followed by relaxed suppers at Royal Lodge.

Sometimes, although she never participated in the water-skiing, the Queen would drive herself from Windsor Castle to Sunninghill. There, nobody ever located the royal party with the exception of one freelance photographer who during the 1960s and 1970s proved the scourge of the Royal Family. He was Ray Bellisario, whose often long-range 'snoop' pictures of intimate royal scenes were bought by the less scrupulous newspapers and magazines. Sunninghill shots were, of course, among them. Some years later, Lord Snowdon, with the Princess at his side reversed into Bellisario's car after the man had dogged their every move at an off-duty visit to a country fair. Though Princess Margaret deplored the accident because their children were in the back of the car, the £20 fine Snowdon had to pay may have seemed worth it in retrospect.

It was at Tony's instigation that he and Princess Margaret began taking holidays abroad. Up to this time members of the immediate Royal Family had always migrated to Balmoral in early August, returning to the official treadmill some six weeks later. Every sovereign since Queen Victoria had trekked north, taking with them their children and closest relations. For the sovereign it was a way of taking a holiday and still being accessible to Government ministers, some of whom were traditionally invited to stay at Balmoral for a few days, but while it was more expedient for the 'head of the firm', as Prince Philip once put it, to remain relatively close at hand, princes and princesses were not under a similar obligation to maintain the British holiday tradition.

In March 1963 Princess Margaret and Lord Snowdon broke the pattern and visited Davos in Switzerland, where they found themselves besieged by newsmen. Undaunted, at the beginning of September 1963, at the invitation of Sunny Blandford's sister-in-law, Eugénie Niarchos, they flew to Greece. Their holiday destination was the Niarchos island, Spetsopoula, where the shipping tycoon proved the most generous of hosts.

For newspaper reporters, the novelty of the couple's foreign holidays provided a bonus worthy of their expense accounts, even if the Princess's 'business trips' to Germany earlier in the year had aroused little interest. In March, as honorary colonel, she had visited Münster to inspect the 15th/19th King's Royal Hussars, and in July a visit to the 1st Battalion Royal Highland Fusiliers and a tour of the N.A.T.O. air base had taken her to Brüggen.

During October, confirmation that Princess Margaret was expecting a baby the following spring meant a gradual winding down of her public appearances. In fact the spring of 1964 promised a rich crop of royal offspring. So many royal babies had not been expected since the so-called 'succession stakes' of 1818-19 when, to provide the throne with an heir – a British-born heir – George III's sons rallied to Parliament's call in the wake of the death of the Prince Regent's only child, Princess Charlotte Augusta of Wales. More than a century later, though the line of succession was not in jeopardy, the Queen was expecting her fourth child, Princess Margaret, like the Duchess of Kent, her second, and Princess Alexandra, who had married the year before, was expecting her first.

On Saturday 1 May 1964, Princess Margaret gave birth to a daughter at Kensington Palace. In their garden, against the white cast-iron pergola (once part of the iron stand at Ascot), the Princess and Lord Snowdon planted a climbing red rose to commemorate the occasion. Ten weeks later, on 13 July, the child received the names Sarah Frances Elizabeth at her christening in the private chapel at Buckingham Palace. Her five godparents were Jocelyn Stevens' wife Jane and his step-sister Prudence Penn, Marigold Bridgeman, Lord Westmorland and Anthony Barton.

The reception in the Queen's Gallery following the ceremony was a congenial, light-hearted affair. But like the happy scenes – witnessed by the press in Clock Court as the Snowdon family left home beforehand – the proud smiles worn by both Princess Margaret and her husband already belied Tony's changing attitude to his wife and his situation. So unexpected was his treatment of the Princess, in fact, that he had begun to reveal characteristics which not only took her by surprise but literally by storm. Indeed, during the early months of 1964, Princess Margaret's doctor expressed concern over the effects that her distress might cause her pregnancy.

Whatever had started to go wrong – and clearly something had – matters seemed to have improved by the time Princess Margaret and Tony flew out of England the following month bound for Sardinia. Their host for the first part of their holiday was the young Aga Khan, Prince Karim, known to his friends simply as 'K'. Regarded by Ismailis as their Imam or spiritual leader, the Aga Khan, reputed to be descended from Muhammad's son-in-law, was in the process of launching a fabulous holiday resort on the Costa Smeralda, said to have cost eighty million pounds. The resort was to provide Princess Margaret and Lord Snowdon with a brief, utopian sojourn, during which the world would be alerted to the holiday spot's existence.

The Princess and her husband stayed at the Hotel Pitrizza, from where they swam, water-skied, or cruised aboard the Aga Khan's yacht, the *Amaloun*. It was while cruising to the island of Sofia, a few days after her thirty-fourth birthday, that Princess Margaret found herself at the centre of a much publicized scare. The *Amaloun* hit a rock and as the stern sank the Princess and her party climbed into a dinghy. Snowdon, in the meantime, had climbed aloft to untie another dinghy before diving into the sea. They were all eventually rescued by people who were cruising on a large yacht nearby.

At the end of August the couple moved on from Sardinia to Italy and the 'cultural' part of their holiday. The Princess thought it a good idea that in Sardinia they should do nothing but unwind and enjoy the sun and the sea, but in Italy, where they were joined by Jocelyn and Jane Stevens at the Villa Malcontenta near Venice, which had been lent to Lord Snowdon, they should spend most of their time sight-seeing.

'I called Princess Margaret "the Master Planner",' says Jocelyn Stevens. 'She loved planning what we were going to do and she keeps the most marvellous albums which she faithfully writes up. At the end of each day she would write out her notes, asking us what we had seen. She knew perfectly well, of course, but she wanted to make sure we had noticed as much as she had.

'It was like being debriefed. We'd all sit in the corner, pretending to be tired or bored, but she took it all very seriously. She loved it. It was the most *marvellous* holiday and she and Tony got on so well.'

The Princess and Lord Snowdon were hardly back in Britain that summer before they were flying out again. This time on an official nine-day duty visit to Denmark for British Week. 1965 opened with more travel when they made a short, private visit to Ireland to see Lord Snowdon's sister Susan, Viscountess de Vesci, at her family's home at Abbey Leix.

On their first day there, IRA sympathizers made it known that the British Princess, even as an unofficial visitor, was not welcome. Crude posters demanded 'Go Home Maggie!' and 'Down With The Queen!', while leaflets urged supporters, 'Show your hostility!' Some did. A tree was felled and dragged across a road to block their way, and bicycle chains were hurled at the electric cables to the house. According to Princess Margaret the result of this was that the town of Abbey Leix and not the de Vesci's house, which had its own generator, was plunged into darkness.

Yet while the antagonistic sentiments of some had been made clear, the more general feeling at the Snowdons' presence – as on earlier visits – was one of pleasure. This was seen in the warmth of a demonstration on the day the Princess and her husband returned to London. For reasons of security, they had been advised to fly from Dublin airport and not Shannon. The Guarda further instructed that, because they could not vouch for the safety of the VIP lounge at Dublin, they were to be escorted direct to their aircraft by a car marked 'Follow Me'. Princess Margaret recalls that as they approached the airport, 'The streets were lined with thousands of people who were all cheering and calling out "Come back again".'

At no time, however, did they encounter the specially marked escort car, which meant they found themselves on the wrong side of the airport barrier, and instantly engulfed by the crowd. So keen were those waiting to see the couple that they broke spontaneously into choruses of 'For She's a Jolly Good Fellow', all the while trying to lift her car off the ground. The Princess was astounded, especially when 'they started thumping on the roof'. The only solution was for the couple to get out and make their way to the very lounge they had been warned not to go near. Princess Margaret remembers, 'Everybody was telling me not to worry and to come back soon.' Somebody called from the crowd, 'Next time bring your mother,' 'And tell her to bring the horse,' yelled somebody else. 'What if it doesn't win?' asked the Princess. 'It will ... we'll carry it round,' came back the reply.

Of the special 'Follow Me' vehicle, the Princess learned that it had led what the driver thought was the royal car safely on to the tarmac, only to discover that it contained two very perplexed Americans, protesting that they did not want to go to London but back home to the United States.

Two months later there was another change of mood and climate as Princess Margaret and her husband paid an official visit to Uganda. At Kampala, they received an enthusiastic welcome from the Kabaka of Buganda, known as King Freddie, and his Prime Minister Dr Milton Obote. The tour was another to Princess Margaret's credit, both personally and diplomatically, and the Kabaka and his Prime

Minister did well to enjoy it too, for, as history relates, Dr Obote ousted King Freddie – who fled to England, where he died in penury not long afterwards – and in time, Obote himself was ousted by Idi Amin.

Altogether 1965 was a particularly busy year for Princess Margaret and Tony, both individually and together. Public duties increased and were packed around official and unofficial visits abroad. Lord Snowdon was increasingly taken up with his own professional commitments, including the preparation of a new photographic book entitled *Private View*. Manned by Dorothy Everard, who had been his secretary-assistant for a number of years, his office seemed almost as busy as the Princess's on the other side of the courtyard and was fast becoming a volatile area, as Snowdon grew irritable at having to 'fit in' with his wife's engagements.

However, one of the couple's official engagements Tony did not object to was an American tour planned for the Princess and her husband in the autumn of 1965. Tony had been there before but the Princess had not, and despite her marital difficulties it was an experience she looked forward to with pleasure and not a little excitement. Before that, however, there was more than enough to keep them occupied on this side of the Atlantic. Included among their engagements that spring was another British Fair, this time in the Netherlands, and, more privately, the celebration of the Queen's thirty-ninth birthday on 21 April. To mark the occasion, Princess Margaret and Lord Snowdon took the Queen and the Duke of Edinburgh to an evening performance of Spike Milligan's show, *Son of Oblomov*. Later, Milligan joined the Princess, her husband and their party at Kensington Palace. There he found fellow 'Goon' Peter Sellers, and his wife, the Swedish starlet Britt Ekland, who had become good friends of the Princess and Tony. So friendly were they at this time that, with Jocelyn and Jane Stevens, they had starred in a home movie, complete with sound-track.

One scene with Princess Margaret and Peter Sellers ran:

SELLERS: I am going to impersonate Her Royal Highness Princess Margaret.
[Disappears behind a screen, over the top of which are thrown items of clothing. From behind the screen appears Princess Margaret who curtseys and steps back again.]
[Peter Sellers steps out.]

SELLERS: I am now going to impersonate Queen Victoria.
[Disappears behind the screen once more. Moments later he steps out dressed normally.]
SELLERS: I don't know what Queen Victoria looked like.

By the time the summer round of public functions had drawn to a close, Princess Margaret and Lord Snowdon were ready for another holiday on the Costa Smeralda. In fact the resort was to see them several times during the closing years of the decade, but that they were there one year and suddenly not the next, gave rise to a story that the Princess had fallen out with the Aga Khan after he had ignored a birthday dinner party given in the Princess's honour. Princess Margaret dismissed the story as yet more wearisome press invention. 'He didn't ignore it,' she says, 'he *gave* the party.'

Up to this point, although it was becoming increasingly apparent that all was far from well between them, Princess Margaret and Tony had enjoyed their holiday. The Princess tried hard not to be frightened by whatever it was that was gnawing away at her husband, even though she did not find it easy.

Jocelyn and Jane Stevens noticed the change in Tony when they joined the couple near Brindisi for the last leg of their Italian holiday. They stayed for a few days in the thirteenth-century castle in Oria and then motored up to Rome. There the party met up with Judy Montagu and her husband, the American writer and art critic Milton Gendel, who put his studio-cum-office at the royal couple's disposal. But while Princess Margaret liked the idea, Lord Snowdon did not. He wanted them all to stay together and began sulking. When the Princess attempted to placate him, he fell into a prolonged silence which continued throughout the following morning. Then, to make certain that his displeasure had not gone unnoticed by Princess Margaret, Tony climbed out of a window and up on to the roof. It was there, a little later, that Jocelyn Stevens found him, sitting cross-legged on a flat-topped chimney.

In his biography of Lord Snowdon, David Sinclair provides some insight into his subject's behaviour: 'Snowdon recognized the dilemma inherent in his position and dealt with it by resolutely following his own instincts, as those who knew him well had foreseen he would do. "I am not a member of the Royal Family, I am married to a member of the Royal Family",' Snowdon always said.

Nevertheless, there were obviously problems over reconciling the different aspects of his life. On the one hand he could not escape his role as Princess Margaret's consort and on the other he fully intended to pursue his career and all that this entailed. In short, he wanted the best of both worlds.

'Snowdon himself, of course, could not remain untouched by these conflicting images. "I think his involvement with the Royal Family caused problems for him in the way he was expected to behave by people," says a long-time acquaintance. ... One gets the impression that he believed he should have been able to wear his royal aura like an overcoat, taking it off when it became inconvenient or restricted his freedom of movement.'

'It could not be said that Princess Margaret was to blame for the problems,' Sinclair went on. '... Indeed, the idea of blame in such circumstances is probably invalid – we are all prisoners of our personalities.'

Be that as it may, the change in Lord Snowdon was unnerving. He was now frequently vindictive; wanting, yet at the same time, resisting the Princess. By her own admission, he was no longer the man she had married. He had withdrawn his support and was destroying the peace and harmony of their home life which Princess Margaret felt acutely. In many ways, it was as though she were now married to a stranger.

CHAPTER ELEVEN

FACTS AND FICTIONS

On the morning of 4 November 1965, Princess Margaret and Lord Snowdon set out for America. As the Princess's car drove through the gates of Kensington Palace, a handful of onlookers, including a passing clergyman, called out *bon voyage* and messages of goodwill. The Princess waved, while her husband called back thanks through an open window. Goodwill was to be found in small measure elsewhere, however. Willie Hamilton MP seized the opportunity to jump on his favourite hobby-horse from where he lambasted the Princess and what he saw as the reasons behind her trip.

His objections – hardly mellowed by time – later found their way into a book (*My Queen and I*, 1975), where he wrote: 'For long it had been known that Princess Margaret was keen to see the pop culture of the States, but her wishes had come to naught. By the early summer of 1965 her persistence paid off when she suggested that, if she attended two functions organized by the English Speaking Union, and two fashion shows laid on by the Incorporated Society of London Fashion Designers, in San Francisco and Los Angeles, the Foreign Office might plausibly foot the bill. The Labour Foreign Secretary, Mr Michael Stewart, yielded to these blandishments.'

Then, quoting from something he called 'the propagandist hand-out prepared by *Labour* Ministers' (his italics), he added that 'during the entire tour of three weeks the total time spent on official engagements was under forty-eight hours'. An inspection of Princess Margaret's itinerary (Appendix IV), however, gives no indication that this was a thinly veiled pleasure trip, but it does serve to weaken considerably Willie Hamilton's argument.

For the Princess and Lord Snowdon, it was an exciting but exhausting tour, during which they fulfilled over eighty engagements of an official, semi-official and private nature, toured five cities and were entertained by more or less everybody who was anybody. 'I enjoyed it all enormously,' Princess Margaret says, 'and I have kept an abiding love for the United States ever since. I like to go back whenever I can.' It is extremely doubtful, however, that either Princess Margaret or her husband had sufficient time during this particular visit to become acquainted with America's so-called 'pop culture', as their critics suggested. One perplexed American journalist, for example, asked the Princess why she had chosen to visit the laboratories of the California Institute of Technology and not Disneyland. 'Because I'm more interested in technology,' she replied. Be that as it may, there was more than a touch of glamour to this tour and it was this aspect that drew the most attention.

Visiting the lot of Universal Studios in north Hollywood, a private though well-publicized function, doubtless seemed more newsworthy than watching the Princess inspect British displays in Fifth Avenue stores. A tramcar ride in San Francisco was more picturesque than watching a ceremony in Arlington Cemetery, at which the Princess laid a wreath on the grave of President Kennedy. And the media was more curious about a private party given by Mrs Katzenbach – considered to be the American 'Hostess with the Mostest' – than the royal visit to a working session of the United Nations.

Then came the high-spot; a White House reception given by President Lyndon B. Johnson. Guests told Princess Margaret that it was the first party of its kind in the White House since the Kennedys had left. And as those present said afterwards, the reception had not only been greatly appreciated and enjoyed, but the Snowdons had received the type of publicity that other figures in the public eye would have had to pay millions for. The Princess's evening with the President of course totally overshadowed her visit to open the British Fair organized by the Daughters of the British Empire.

However, even the most hostile critics could not overlook the fact that Princess Margaret and Lord Snowdon had been to America to 'show the flag' and had done so with a professionalism difficult to fault. As comedian Bob Hope told a distinguished audience at the World Adoption International Fund Ball, 'Everyone is conscious of the Royal couple's visit. I waved at a traffic cop and he curtsied back.'

With the American visit at an end, the Princess and her husband flew to Bermuda, where Her Royal Highness presented Colours to the Bermuda Regiment at the National Stadium. A cocktail party followed a tree-planting ceremony in the grounds of Government House and an official dinner followed by a reception for 120 guests wound up their lightning visit to the island. Then, at a minute before midnight, Princess Margaret and Lord Snowdon climbed aboard their London-bound aircraft.

The following spring, Anglo-American relations were once more at the heart of another of Princess Margaret's foreign visits. In Nice she and Lord Snowdon officially attended a ball to celebrate the sixtieth anniversary of the British-American Hospital. The evening itself was a resounding success, even if very little was said about it in the press at home. But when a civic lunch ran over time, delaying the couple's arrival in Cannes – where they were to see the British entry at the annual Film Festival – they were booed by the audience for being late, all of which was leapt upon by the hordes of journalists present. The Princess recalls that the only warm welcome she received was from the film actress Sophia Loren. 'We're all so hot and so late ...' she sympathized. Shaken, and not a little miffed at the experience – 'I'd never been booed before ...' – Princess Margaret felt like walking out. Lord Snowdon, however, told her to remain where she was and promptly went out to explain to the press the reasons for the delay.

A more tranquil and traditional scene was witnessed in London the following month, when Princess Margaret drove from Clarence House to the City Guildhall in an open landau, escorted by a Captain's Escort of the Household Cavalry. For some years she had declined to accept the Freedom of the City of London on the grounds that she was 'not worthy of that honour', but the City's persistence had finally won her round. During the ceremony, the Princess often glanced up to the gallery where her five-year-old son, David, sat with his nanny, Miss Verona Sumner, to watch the pageant below.

At about this time Princess Margaret was fired with great enthusiasm over plans to build a country retreat at Sunninghill, near Windsor Great Park. She believed that Tony would share her enthusiasm, but she was mistaken. Instead, he had in mind the renovation of an old cottage on the Nymans estate at Handcross in Sussex. Old House, as it is known, had belonged to Snowdon's grandmother, and it was there that the Messel family used to picnic. It was not Princess Margaret's idea of heaven, however, not merely because it was situated in a field and inaccessible by road, but, she says 'because it was haunted'. In any event, she was adamant that she did not want to live in a house, not even a weekend retreat, that she and Tony had not planned together. Ideally she wanted somewhere that would be *theirs*.

Failing to reach an agreement, the couple called in their business manager to act as arbiter. He considered the matter carefully, weighing up the pros and cons of both locations, and came to the conclusion that Sunninghill, for a number of reasons, was the better proposition. Snowdon deferred to this decision and agreed that he and the Princess should go ahead with plans for it. But the planning did not get anywhere and, taking a step that can only be seen as a clear case of territorial imperative, Tony went ahead with the costly renovation of Old House behind his wife's back. In her own words, Princess Margaret 'was crushed' by his disregard of the agreement so recently reached. The house at Sunninghill never materialized and this episode caused serious damage to the Snowdons' marital relationship. To make matters even more awkward, Tony now ensured that events were given an extra and rather curious twist, which resulted in a classic situation, recognizable to countless husbands and wives.

Princess Margaret had always hated Tony's frequent absences from home and made her feelings known. He therefore started inviting a friend from his Cambridge days to keep the Princess company. By throwing them together Snowdon may have been trying to justify his own interest in other women. Yet, paradoxically it was not long before Tony started to resent the relationships between his wife and other men. He was to resent, and suspect, for example, her friendship with Robin Douglas-Home who was, says the Princess, 'a musical friend', somebody with whom she could share her interest. Tony believed it went further than that and would not be persuaded otherwise. But then he was never able to understand that his wife had male friends with whom she enjoyed a close rapport.

Disciples of the movement for women's liberation would probably see this as male chauvinism. Yet ironically Princess Margaret had never wanted, much less envisaged, the type of 'open' marriage she was now a party to. On the other hand, as a thirty-five-year-old woman, possessing both looks and intelligence, and having a great liking for people, she could hardly be expected to abandon herself to a life of emptiness.

To the public at large, however, in spite of frequent rumours, the Princess and Lord Snowdon appeared happy enough together, and this was precisely the image it was vital for them to present to the world. Equally vital, as Princess Margaret made plain to her husband, was the well-being of their children. This she considered paramount, reminding Tony that the break-up of his parents' marriage had resulted in an often strained relationship with them in later years.

If, however, the couple hoped to keep their troubles away from the press indefinitely, they were soon to be disappointed. For on Monday 27 February 1967, the front page of the London *Daily Express* announced 'Tony Denies Rift With Margaret'. From New York, Henry Lowrie, the paper's correspondent, filed a report which began: 'Lord Snowdon tonight denied reports in American papers about a rift between him and Princess Margaret.... He arrived in New York from Tokyo to find newspapers here carrying front-page stories of a "break-up". He was "amazed". To reporters, Lord Snowdon said, "Nothing has happened to our marriage. When I am away – and I'm away quite a lot on assignments for my paper – I write home and I telephone like other husbands in love with their wives. I telephoned today." He later added, "I can't understand what started this, but some of these papers have been hinting about this since six months after my marriage. No responsible journalist could possibly take seriously such silly stories." '

Snowdon was right in mentioning premature rumours that his marriage had run into difficulties during its first year, but he was attempting to pull the wool over a great many people's eyes by mentioning his consideration for his wife. 'He never rang or wrote when he was abroad,' Princess Margaret tells one, 'which made it awkward when friends asked for news of him.' At first she made excuses, pressure of work and so on, but in the end the Princess was forced to admit that she never heard from him when he was away.

Hardly a newspaper did not carry the rift story in Britain that day, and even *The Times* ran an item, though under a less prominent headline. Princess Margaret, of course, remained silent. But that evening, there were doubtless many who were now more curious than ever to have a look at her as she arrived in driving rain for that year's Royal Film Performance. The film chosen to be honoured was Franco Zeffirelli's interpretation of Shakespeare's *The Taming of the Shrew*.

In the line-up of stars to be presented to the Princess, looking glamorous in a long, slim dress of silver, and a turquoise and diamond tiara set on her elaborately dressed hair, were the film's leading players, Richard Burton and Elizabeth Taylor. Princess Margaret talked to them for some minutes before taking her seat in the circle. A little later, from the stage of the Odeon Cinema in Leicester Square, Burton told the kind of story that had rung through Princess Margaret's ears so often that her smile was now more of a civil gesture, but which that night was tinged with irony.

'My name,' he said, 'is really Richard Jenkins, therefore my wife is Liz Jenkins. And up there is a young lady whose real name is Maggie Jones.'

In the meantime, Lord Snowdon remained in New York, working on some of the four thousand photographs he had taken in Japan. 'There is no question of my trying to hide,' he had said. 'I just must be able to work as an ordinary journalist.' There was not in fact any reason for him to hide. In any event Princess Margaret had arranged to meet him there on 10 March, en route to the Bahamas. They met up that day as the Princess changed aircraft in New York and they embraced and talked together as though neither had a care in the world. Upon their arrival in the Bahamas they smiled through an official welcoming ceremony, climbed into a waiting limousine and, with an escort of police outriders, made off in the direction of Lyford Cay where they were to stay with Jocelyn and Jane Stevens.

On the way Snowdon was struck by an idea that would recall happier days. Asking their chauffeur to stop the car, Tony got out and approached a bemused outrider, who agreed to swap places with them. Then, mounting the police motorbike – Tony driving and Princess Margaret riding pillion – they roared off into the distance, leaving the convoy to follow at its own pace. For the Princess and her husband the holiday was to continue quite like old times; their 'togetherness' was unmistakeable. At home in Britain, photographs of them strolling arm-in-arm along a wooden pier were intended to prove that the widely discussed 'rift' was not all it may have seemed.

That autumn the royal couple were scheduled to pay a three-day visit to Brussels for yet another British Week before they both flew on to Ottawa to visit a hospital named after the Princess and to tour the 'Expo '67' complex at Montreal. To mark these events, a new set of photographs of the Princess were taken by Tony. Part in light, part in shadow, more alluring studies of her had not been seen for a number of years. 'Normally, official photographs are taken before any big occasion,' explained the Princess's press secretary, 'and this time, Lord Snowdon, who will be accompanying his wife to Belgium, decided to take them. After all [he added diplomatically] she is his favourite subject.'

The night before their scheduled departure at the beginning of October the embargo placed on the new photographs was lifted and, the following day, they were reproduced in the national press. Then at the eleventh hour, came a disappointing blow to those who had organized the opening ceremony. Lord Snowdon, it was announced, would be going to Brussels alone, deputizing for Princess Margaret who, it was said, though very much to her chagrin, was laid up in bed at Kensington Palace with 'a chill'.

'Can you believe it?' the Princess asks. 'I never cancel engagements because of a chill!' What she had, in fact, was a quinsy (inflammation of the throat with an abscess on or in the region of the tonsils). When it finally cleared, she flew out to join her husband, after being advised by her doctors that she should have an operation for the removal of her tonsils – no small matter for an adult.

The operation was carried out early the following year, after which Princess Margaret flew to Barbados for a short recuperative holiday with Snowdon's uncle, Oliver Messel, who for reasons of his own health had decided to live permanently in the West Indies. By this time, Princess Margaret was also in a position to visit Mustique. While facilities there were still very basic, Colin Tennant had begun a programme of development, which meant that the Princess could think seriously about building on the plot of land she had been given as a wedding present nearly eight years before.

She hoped that her proposals for a house on the island might prove a productive alternative to the Sunninghill/Old House episode. But in this she was wrong and history began to repeat itself. Tony flatly refused to have anything to do with Mustique. He similarly refused his wife's invitation to design what she hoped might have become *their* house. So the Princess turned instead to Oliver Messel.

The plot of land Princess Margaret had been given occupied a headland just big enough for a house and a small tropical garden. A mass of dense, thorny vegetation cloaked the steep slope down to the coves and lagoons of Gelliceaux Bay below, and it was after the bay itself that the Princess decided to name her house, the first she had ever owned in her own right. Not taking the local spelling 'Gelliceaux', she reverted to the correct French name of Les Jolies Eaux, meaning pretty waters.

Oliver Messel's final plans for the one-level house materialized in a U-shaped building built from locally quarried stone and set round three sides of a paved courtyard. Central to the design is the south-facing sitting-room which, when the doors are all folded back, is completely open to the air. Occupying the breadth of the house, this area is flanked by two short wings which contain the kitchen and four bedrooms. Steps lead away from the terrace to a small patch of lawn leading down to the swimming-pool and beyond that stands a wooden gazebo with a palm-thatched roof.

After a good deal of hard work the house was ready for occupation, and the Princess complemented the magnificent seascape with a simple, relaxed interior. Pale green walls frame the blue panorama beyond and the modern furniture, some of it bamboo, is chosen for comfort. The spectacular view stretches across a clear expanse of ocean towards the neighbouring islands, including Petite Mustique. Les Jolies Eaux was, not surprisingly, to become Princess Margaret's own private haven and to add a new dimension to her life.

By now Lord Snowdon had also begun to tread new ground. Branching away from stills photography to film-making, he was commissioned by the Columbia Broadcasting System (C.B.S.), one of America's top television networks, to make a documentary about old age. *Don't Count the Candles* received its first showing in the United States in March 1968, and in early April it was transmitted in Britain by the B.B.C. Its harrowing brilliance was undeniable. So loudly applauded was it that the film ran away with no fewer than five trophies: two Emmy awards from Hollywood, the San Giorgio Prize at the Venice Film Festival and two further awards from Prague and Barcelona. This was the first in a series of films Lord Snowdon was to make which received wide acclaim and pricked at people's social consciences.

His involvement with the disabled – which continues to this day – also stemmed from this period, when he became a member of the Committee of the National Fund for Research into Crippling Diseases. Shortly afterwards his first contribution to the improvement of wheelchairs was launched. Snowdon's invention has been described as not 'a wheelchair at all, but a brilliant motive power pack that could be fitted to an ordinary chair or even a high stool and give the user considerably greater mobility than the conventional model allowed'. The crippled journalist Quentin Crewe was presented with Tony's first fully operational model. 'There are some things,' wrote Crewe, 'which are recognized as great leaps in imagination. This platform seems to me to be one of them.' Four years later a more sophisticated version of Snowdon's invention – now known commercially as the Chairmobile – was manufactured, retailing at a little under £100.

From the improvement of wheelchairs, Lord Snowdon turned to invalid cars, machines which he considered 'intrinsically lethal'. This was the topic of his maiden speech in the House of Lords in 1974 and during the same year he and writer Adam Fergusson put their heads together to produce a report for *The Times* on the hazards of invalid cars. The Snowdon/Fergusson article doubtless helped push the Government into reconsidering its stance on the mobility of the disabled.

To his list of credits as a photographer, film-maker, designer and inventor, Lord Snowdon could also add that of director of royal ceremonial. In 1958, at the time of the British Empire and Commonwealth Games in Cardiff, the Queen had announced that she intended to create her son Charles, Prince of Wales: 'When he is grown up,' she told the Welsh people, 'I will present him to you at Caernarvon'. The Prince's Investiture took place eleven years later on 1 July 1969, after well over a year spent planning the event. While the Duke of Norfolk, as Earl Marshal, was responsible overall, Snowdon, who had been made Constable of Caernarvon Castle in

1963, took control as designer-in-chief. And since the entire pageant was to prove a feat of the highest theatricality, who better to figure at the very heart of its organization? On top of the personal satisfaction that Snowdon must have felt at the close of the day, he received a reward of thanks from the Queen, who invested her brother-in-law with the GCVO; the Knight Grand Cross Victorian Order.

For Princess Margaret and her husband, a final tour together brought the sixties full circle. Leaving London on Friday 19 September, the Snowdons were to be away for three weeks visiting Japan, Hong Kong, Cambodia, Thailand and Iran. The tour, linked by nine flights, included ninety-eight official engagements, among them the inspection of twenty-three exhibitions (or displays), thirteen dinner and eight luncheon appointments, and eight formal receptions (one of which was attended by 3,000 guests). They were to make two journeys aboard the famous Japanese 'bullet' trains and pay formal visits to four temples and three mosques.

Of the entire tour, the nine-day Japanese progress was by far the most hectic, with each day's programme starting early and frequently continuing into the small hours of the following morning. That on which Princess Margaret inaugurated British Week in Tokyo provides some idea of the type of day the Princess has undertaken on many tours, and it is perhaps worthwhile to reproduce the royal schedule for Friday 26 September 1969, bearing in mind that events like these are rarely reported in the British national press.

9.23 a.m.   Princess Margaret and Lord Snowdon leave the [British] Embassy and at . . .

9.26 a.m.   arrive at the National Theatre and join other members of the Platform Party for the Opening Ceremony of British Week.

9.27 a.m.   Her Imperial Highness The Princess Chichibu arrives.

9.28 a.m.   The Platform Party proceeds into the National Theatre and at . . .

9.30 a.m.   the Opening Ceremony begins.

9.50 a.m.   The Opening Ceremony ends. Her Royal Highness and the Platform Party proceed to a waiting-room, while the other guests assemble outside the theatre.

10.00 a.m.	Princess Margaret assists at the release of balloons.
10.05 a.m.	Her Royal Highness and Lord Snowdon leave the National Theatre and at . . .
10.10 a.m.	arrive at the Nippon Budokan in order to view British cars displayed outside and meet officials concerned with the 'Britain in Tokyo' Exhibition.
10.25 a.m.	Her Royal Highness cuts the ribbon opening the 'Britain in Tokyo' Exhibition and together with Lord Snowdon tours the exhibits.
11.15 a.m.	Her Royal Highness and Lord Snowdon accompanied by the Ambassador leave the Budokan and at . . .
11.18 a.m.	arrive at the Science Museum in order to tour the British Instrument and Aerospace Exhibitions.
11.55 a.m.	Her Royal Highness and Lord Snowdon accompanied by the Ambassador leave the Science Museum and at . . .
12.00 p.m.	return to the Embassy.
12.43 p.m.	Her Royal Highness and Lord Snowdon leave the Embassy and at . . .
12.50 p.m.	arrive at the Hotel Okura.
1.00 p.m.	Her Royal Highness and Lord Snowdon attend the Opening Day Luncheon for the Committe of Honour (100 guests).
2.40 p.m.	Her Royal Highness leaves the Hotel Okura.
2.50 p.m.	Lord Snowdon leaves the Hotel Okura.
3.00 p.m.	Her Royal Highness arrives at Seibu Department Store, Ikebukuro.
3.00 p.m.	Lord Snowdon arrives at the Sony Building, Ginza, to open the Hi-Fi and Home Appliances Show.
3.30 p.m.	Lord Snowdon leaves the Sony Building.
3.40 p.m.	Her Royal Highness leaves Seibu and at . . .
3.45 p.m.	arrives at Tobu Department Store.
3.45 p.m.	Lord Snowdon arrives at the British Council in order to view the British Book Display Centre.
4.05 p.m.	Her Royal Highness leaves Tobu.
4.15 p.m.	Lord Snowdon leaves the British Council.
4.25 p.m.	Her Royal Highness arrives at Mitsukoshi Department Store, Nihombashi.

4.30 p.m.	Lord Snowdon arrives at Mitsukoshi Department Store.
5.20 p.m.	Her Royal Highness and Lord Snowdon leave the Store and at ...
5.30 p.m.	return to the Embassy.
7.48 p.m.	Her Royal Highness and Lord Snowdon join the other guests for a dinner at the Embassy (30 guests).
8.00 p.m.	Dinner at the Embassy.
9.30 p.m.	Her Royal Highness retires and at ...
9.40 p.m.	The Princess and Lord Snowdon join other guests for a Reception at the Embassy (250 guests).

For Princess Margaret and Lord Snowdon the early 1970s were years of rapid marital decline. If he was at home during the day, Snowdon locked himself in his study, only to venture out at night. Most often he would not return until morning. And, if, for example, the Princess and Tony should happen to pass in the hall of their house at Kensington Palace, a grunt was the response the Princess came to expect to anything she said. For the most part she encountered nothing but a heavy silence 'like a brick wall', or occasionally would discover antagonistic notes left on her writing table. There had been times, too, when Snowdon delighted in belittling the Princess in front of guests or in hurling her royal rank back at her without reason. Friends who had often witnessed Tony's behaviour told Princess Margaret they believed that his disturbing outbursts were calculated to unsettle her.

For years the Princess, who admits to a rather 'Edwardian attitude' towards marriage, had tried to overlook the ugliness of such incidents in the belief that it was all part of a husband's normal pattern of behaviour. Still she tried to hold the marriage together even though, as time passed, she began to question her own belief in it and found herself not only viewing any warm overtures with suspicion, but battling with an almost constant fear that troubled her until the day she and Lord Snowdon parted.

By the end of 1973 private tension was clearly mirrored in the marked physical change that had taken place in the Princess. In different circumstances, the transition from youth to maturity would almost certainly have been less dramatic. As it was Princess Margaret

began to resemble the famous likenesses of her portly Hanoverian
forebears. Equally unmistakeable – particularly when she was caught
off-guard, or off-duty – was the hunted look of a woman in despair.

Yet still the Princess and Lord Snowdon were obliged to maintain
appearances, even though the inevitable recriminations made this
increasingly difficult. To all intents and purposes the couple had
started to lead separate lives, but until this was formally recognized,
and all pretence could cease, Lord Snowdon had to accompany his
wife on some of her official engagements as part of the façade. In
May 1973, following her visit to the Virgin Islands, Tony accompanied the Princess to Florence for the opening of an exhibition of
work by Henry Moore. While there they stayed as the guests of Sir
Harold Acton at his house in Tuscany, where local students came to
present one of their hats to the Princess, just as their predecessors had
done in 1949.

Later that summer, taking their children with them, the Snowdons returned to Italy on what proved to be their last holiday
together. It was a disaster, for no sooner had they arrived than Tony
fell into one of his silences. 'Papa, Mummy is talking to you,' one of
the children would say. 'I know,' was all he replied. Then, at the
end of the first week, as the Princess recalls, Snowdon packed his
bag and returned to London, leaving her with David and Sarah to
continue their holiday alone.

In other circles, divorce would have been the natural sequel. It has
even been said that Princess Margaret had been seeking the dissolu-
tion of her marriage since 1970, but this she had not. Indeed the
possiblity was ruled out for the simple reasons that she neither
wanted nor approved of divorce. Meanwhile, throughout this
period the Queen had been watching her sister anxiously, trying to
offer whatever advice she could, while trying to keep peace with
her brother-in-law, who frequently off-loaded his troubles on her.

The following spring, Princess Margaret was able to take a brief
respite from the atmosphere at home. She had been invited to visit
Barbados in order to open British Week and from there she would
fly on to Mustique where Les Jolies Eaux, now completed, awaited
her.

From then on the Princess established a pattern of visiting the
island twice a year if she possibly could: in February, when most
members of the Royal Family take the opportunity to holiday

abroad (it is always a particularly quiet time in their official lives), and again in the late autumn. But while the winter holidays enjoyed by her relations escaped criticism, Princess Margaret's did not. Criticism aside, however, the most curious stories to emerge were that her winter sorties to Mustique were primarily prompted by reasons of health.

Throughout her life Princess Margaret has been dogged by stories that she does not enjoy the rudest of constitutions. Colds, chills, influenza, the occasional bout of tonsillitis and migraine (from which she no longer suffers) have been cited as evidence and considerably overplayed. It may safely be said, however, that, while the Princess is susceptible to stomach trouble, she has suffered from such common ailments no more than any other mortal. Indeed as one of her intimates has put it, 'She's as tough as boots.'

The most fantastic of the assertions concerning the Princess's health was made in 1978 by the author of a book entitled *Margaret: The Tragic Princess*. In it James Brough devoted an entire chapter to the discussion of 'a royal malady'. To past generations of royalty, this nameless assailant caused greater fear and consternation than haemophilia, the dreaded bleeding disease which attacked a number of royal males. Today 'the royal malady' is identified as porphyria. At its mildest extreme, the disease, which affects the body's metabolism in varying degrees, may cause nothing more sinister than irritability. At its most virulent, it can induce violence and insanity (as probably happened in the case of King George III). How or why it should have applied to Princess Margaret appears to have been based on nothing more than guesswork and the alleged confirmation of an unnamed specialist. On the subject James Brough wrote:

When the troubles of Margaret and Tony ran as a front-page serial, a Fleet Street reporter named Jack Warden, who specialised in covering events in the palace, picked up a lead that promised fresh headlines; he heard that Margaret had inherited porphyria. He relayed the word to his newspaper, and a second reporter, Tom Brown, was assigned to obtain verification.

He approached a British specialist on the subject and was granted an interview. The doctor confirmed what Warden had been told. . . . After answering the newsman's final questions, the expert added one thing more: if the interview were to be written up and appear in print, he would deny ever having talked with Tom Brown. But there were others, familar with porphyria, who began putting together their long-range observations of Margaret and arriving at the same provisional diagnosis.

No further reference need be made to Mr Brough's hypothesis, however, because an incredulous Princess Margaret categorically states, 'I do *not* have porphyria.'

CHAPTER TWELVE

QUI MAL Y PENSE

At the beginning of September 1973 Princess Margaret first met the young man who was to help revive in her some of the *joie de vivre* which events of recent years had dulled. His name was Roderic Llewellyn.

The second son of Lieutenant-Colonel Sir Henry (Harry) Morton Llewellyn and his wife 'Teeny', formerly the Honourable Christine de Saumarez, Roddy was born on 9 October 1947. Behind him – on his mother's side of the family – descent could be traced from Rollo, 1st Duke of Normandy, and no fewer than eight sovereigns, including William the Conqueror and Kings Henry I, II and III, together with such historical characters as John of Gaunt, Duke of Lancaster, and Edmund of Langley, Duke of York.

Sir Harry Llewellyn was a fine horseman and became a British sports hero during the 1952 Helsinki Olympic Games, when he won a gold medal riding the legendary showjumper Foxhunter. It was about this time that Sir Harry purchased Llanvair Grange, a sprawling estate near Abergavenny in South Wales. The house itself, where Princess Margaret was a guest on two or three occasions, is built around a fifteenth- to sixteenth-century farmhouse to which alterations and additions were made in 1780 and 1810 (when a new façade was added) and again as recently as the 1930s.

From here Roddy Llewellyn was sent to be educated at Hawtreys and Shrewsbury, but he completed his schooling with no specific aim in life. To some extent he became a nomad, travelling and working abroad, first going to Aix-en-Provence in France, then South Africa where his de Saumarez grandparents had settled.

Moving on, he worked in a Rhodesian asbestos mine for three months and then toured Uganda and Kenya before returning home.

Princess Margaret first met him at the Café Royal in Edinburgh on 5 September 1973. That year, as in the past, the Princess had accepted an invitation from Lord and Lady Colin Glenconner to join the final week of their summer house-party at Glen, their estate near Innerleithen. This time, however, the Tenants needed an extra man to balance their numbers. At a loss for guests available at short notice during the holiday season, Lord Glenconner rang Mrs Violet Wyndham, his great-aunt by marriage. As a London hostess, 'Aunt Nose', as Mrs Wyndham was known, entertained a great many people, among them Roddy Llewellyn, whom she instantly suggested.

After a series of telephone calls, Roddy was finally located and, although he had never met Princess Margaret or the Tenants before, he summoned his courage and made tracks, as arranged, to Edinburgh. Lord Glenconner had advised him that the party – Princess Margaret, her son David and daughter Sarah, Lady Anne and himself – would arrive at the Café Royal at 1 p.m. There they would lunch before driving on to Glen.

The Princess and Roddy hit it off immediately. At this time Roddy was almost twenty-six: in some ways older, in others younger than his years. The age gap made little difference, for Princess Margaret enjoys the company of younger people and, like her grandmother Queen Mary, is able to establish a natural, easy rapport with the opposite sex. In many ways there was much to recommend Roddy to the Princess: he was entertaining company, with an appealing vulnerability. There can be little doubt, of course, that had it not been for Princess Margaret, Roddy Llewellyn would almost certainly have remained an obscure figure. Reminded that he had earned a certain notoriety, to say nothing of a footnote in royal history books, his reply is invariably, 'I would much rather have been remembered for having painted a marvellous picture.'

What started as a discreet friendship, conducted with the utmost decorum well away from the public's gaze, was finally to explode amid a storm of critical abuse, the like of which Princess Margaret had never experienced before. However, in the autumn of 1973, all that was clear was that Princess Margaret had found some happiness. Five months after their first meeting, Roddy was invited to accompany the Princess to Mustique. While there he put to practical use the one thing he has always admitted to knowing most about – plants. Through trial and error, he laid out and helped maintain a garden at Les Jolies Eaux. Three years later, having graduated from the Merrist Wood Agricultural College in Surrey, Roddy took up landscape gardening professionally.

For Princess Margaret 1974 was a busy year officially, one in which she made formal visits to Cyprus and North America on top of the duties that befell her at home. It was also a year of mixed personal emotions. The Princess and Llewellyn had, of course, become fond of each other. Their closeness meant that they shared the kind of happiness that had been missing from Princess Margaret's life for several years.

In June 1974, two months after she and Roddy returned from the West Indies, the Princess realized that the pretence surrounding her marriage could not continue. There was still no question of divorce; neither party wanted that. But the Princess did want a formal separation. Princess Margaret herself says that she was 'filled with a renewal of spirit, maybe the Holy Spirit' when she told her husband, as they drove to Windsor for the funeral of the Duke of Gloucester on 14 June, that she no longer wished to spend summer holidays with him. Snowdon's response was to acquiesce without argument. After that, the Princess asked him to move out of her house, which he finally did two years later.

In the past, like many mothers perhaps, Queen Elizabeth the Queen Mother had not always been fully conversant with the deeper emotional episodes in her younger daughter's life. During the crucial part of the Townsend issue, she had also been faced with coming to terms with the reality of widowhood when she was only in her early fifties. A decade later, affection for Lord Snowdon meant that her eyes were not fully open to the sad truth of Princess Margaret's marriage and that she was unlikely to adopt anything but a stance in favour of keeping the marriage together.

What her innermost feelings were about Roddy Llewellyn when his existence was brought to her attention, few will ever know with any certainty, but what may be taken as read is that no member of the immediate Royal Family was enamoured of Princess Margaret's new friendship. Even so, their concern for her was no less great and, contrary to press reports soon to appear, no ultimatum along the lines 'Give Roddy up or stand aside' was ever issued to her.

As the end of the first full year of his friendship with the Princess approached, Roddy found himself increasingly engulfed by new experiences and emotions. He needed an opportunity in which to put events in their proper perspective and on the spur of the moment he took himself off to Guernsey and then, as impulsively, to Turkey.

During his absence in that autumn of 1974, Princess Margaret suffered a nervous breakdown 'brought about by Tony's silences and insensitivity'. It was this collapse, though dramatically exaggerated by one of her friends in particular, that gave rise to a story that Princess Margaret had attempted to commit suicide by swallowing a small number of mogadon tablets. The Princess dismissed the idea as completely ridiculous: 'I was so exhausted because of everything that all I wanted to do was sleep . . . and I did, right through to the following afternoon.'

Jocelyn Stevens was one friend who provided the Princess with enormous support at this time. He also refutes stories of attempted suicide. 'It would be totally out of character . . . she loves life too much. She would never do it.'

About a year or so before Roderic Llewellyn entered Princess Margaret's life in 1973, a tall, attractive brunette in her early thirties was introduced to Lord Snowdon. She was Lucy Lindsay-Hogg, the daughter of a textile designer and the former wife of film director Michael Lindsay-Hogg. Brought together by Derek Hart, with whom Tony worked hand-in-glove on his film assignments, Lucy became Snowdon's production assistant and, some time later of course, his wife.

During the early part of 1975 as their relationship gathered momentum, Tony and Lucy were working together on a new film venture in Australia. In June that year, Roddy Llewellyn also embarked on a new project. At the invitation of a handful of friends, he left London to join what has been described as an 'artistic and aristocratic commune' in Wiltshire.

At Surrendell Farm, which had stood abandoned for fifteen years, the group's first task was to make the house habitable, though its prime objective was to make the farm pay for the Parsenn Sally, a restaurant the community had opened in Bath. For Roddy, dreams of self-sufficiency at Surrendell flourished until 1976, when events in his life made it impossible for him to continue. Yet his dreams had run high throughout the period, and had led to Princess Margaret's visit to the commune and the sale – for £6,000 to the *Daily Express* – of a specially posed photograph of its members.

It was perhaps inevitable that Princess Margaret's friendship with Roddy Llewellyn should hit the headlines at some stage, but it is ironic that when it did Lord Snowdon was regarded as the injured husband with no hint of his own relationship with Mrs Lindsay-Hogg being 'leaked' to the press.

This turning point in the Snowdons' lives came early in 1976 when the *News of the World* published an apparently 'intimate' picture of the Princess and Roddy taken during one of their holiday visits to Mustique. The picture was rather hazy, as is generally the case with long-range shots, but it showed the couple in swimming costumes, sitting side by side at a small wooden table. Few would normally have bothered to look twice at such a 'snap', but this one was different. And that was precisely what the newspaper intended: an older woman, the Princess was forty-three, and a younger man, Roddy was then twenty-seven, relaxing *à-deux* in the tropical sunshine. What the published photograph did not reveal, however, was the couple sitting opposite Princess Margaret and Llewellyn: Lord and Lady Coke, friends of the Princess, who had been masked out of the shot.

When the story broke in Britain, Lord Snowdon, said Fleet Street, descended furiously on Buckingham Palace. Alleged to have hurled the offending newspaper at the Queen amid protests that he had been publicly humiliated, he demanded that his marriage to Princess Margaret be formally ended. No such meeting ever took place. For reasons that must now be self-evident, circumstances did not demand it. But upon seeing the photograph, Lord Snowdon did as the Princess had already asked and promptly moved out of Kensington Palace.

On Wednesday 17 March 1976, the *Daily Mirror* proclaimed 'Margaret and Tony Divorce'. Below it, Audrey Whiting, said to be an authority on the Royal Family, told readers, 'Divorce proceedings have begun between Princess Margaret and Lord Snowdon, I am reliably informed'. The *Daily Express* – first off the mark with stories of a 'rift' in 1967 – announced with more reliability, 'Margaret and Tony set to part'; while the midday edition of the London *Evening News* advised with caution, 'Statement on Margaret expected'. That statement was made in an economically worded communiqué issued from Kensington Palace two days later. It read: 'Her Royal Highness The Princess Margaret, Countess of Snowdon, and the Earl of Snowdon have mutually agreed to live apart. The Princess will carry out her public duties and functions unaccompanied by Lord Snowdon. There are no plans for divorce proceedings'.

'The Queen', said Ronald Allison, then Press Secretary to Her Majesty, 'is naturally very sad at what has happened.' But he added, 'There has been no pressure from the Queen on either Princess Margaret or Lord Snowdon to take any particular course.'

Under the terms of the separation, Lord Linley and Lady Sarah, then aged fourteen and eleven respectively, were to remain at Kensington Palace with their mother, while Lord Snowdon, on whom the Princess had agreed to settle a six-figure sum, was to be granted free access to them.

Not long afterwards, press stories claimed that Snowdon had begun his search for a house in London, instructing estate agents to advise him of properties in the region of £80,000. Once his move from the palace had been effected it was arranged that he would stay first at his mother's house in Stafford Terrace, Kensington, and then at the London home of one of his oldest friends, Jeremy Fry. More immediately, however, Lord Snowdon was flying to Sydney where he was to organize an exhibition of his photographs.

The following morning, 20 March, some ten hours after the official statement from London, Snowdon met representatives of the Australian press. 'I am naturally desperately sad in every way that this had to come,' he announced in a voice surprisingly charged with emotion. 'I would just like to say three things: firstly to pray for the understanding of our two children; secondly to wish Princess Margaret every happiness for her future; thirdly to express with the utmost humility my love, admiration and respect I will always have for her sister, her mother and her entire family.'

If the pathos of Lord Snowdon's statement was lost on the cynical, there was undoubtedly a great many people, both at home and abroad, who regarded this penultimate step in the Snowdons' story with genuine sadness. But for the royal couple, parting was the only step now open to them; indeed, it was a step they should have made years before. When at last it came, however, Princess Margaret found herself warmly congratulated by many of her friends.

In the wake of the official communiqué from Kensington Palace, newsmen now trained their sights on the young man who had kept his head well down and had maintained a discreet silence throughout. But the following week, after he had literally been chased into hiding, Roddy Llewellyn issued a carefully worded statement of his own. In it he said: 'I am not prepared to comment on any of the events of last week. I much regret any embarrassment caused to Her Majesty The Queen and the Royal Family for whom I wish to express the greatest respect, admiration and loyalty. . . .' Roddy then went on to plead for privacy, not only for himself but for the other members of the Surrendell community. 'Could we please be permitted by the media, who have besieged us, to carry on with our work and private lives without further interference?'

At Llanvair Grange the same day, Sir Harry Llewellyn, who by now had received a number of offensive letters after media disclosures, described Roddy as 'a young man powerless to defend himself'. At the end of the month, Sir Harry was writing to Roddy in kindly terms, hoping that he would soon quit the commune and expressing his concern that the bad press it had attracted internationally could only do the Royal Family harm and cause embarrassment to his family and friends.

Throughout this entire period the news media treated the Princess's involvement with Roddy Llewellyn as a torridly passionate love affair, something to be admired, ridiculed or even reviled, and in the absence of any explanation to the contrary, press stories were bound to proliferate. Matters were not helped very much by the occasional direct quote from Roddy himself. 'I cannot talk about my feelings for Princess Margaret or her feelings for me,' he told British journalist Harry Arnold. 'That is a taboo subject.'

Yet despite the tantalizing touch of mystery, the truth was much less colourful than the press sensationalism. In short, Princess Margaret and Roddy Llewellyn shared nothing more torrid or passionate than what may be called a loving friendship. It should also be borne in mind that on holiday, such as on Mustique, Roddy was never the Princess's sole house-guest; Lord and Lady Buckhurst, amongst others, were also frequent holiday companions in the Princess's party.

In April during the lull that followed the announcement, Princess Margaret – by now looking slimmer and happier – flew out of Britain to pay official visits to Morocco and Tunisia. In some respects her stay in Morocco may have paved the way for a State Visit the Queen and Prince Philip were to make four years later in 1980. With the approach of Her Majesty's tour, Princess Margaret was said to have warned her sister that the car rides she experienced were like being kidnapped. This time the press was almost right in quoting the Princess, but not quite. '*Like* being kidnapped?' she says. 'I was abducted by the King . . . which I enjoyed enormously.'

Unexpected though it was, the incident had its amusing side. Scheduled to dine with the King or the 'despotic Hassan' (as some preferred to call him during the Queen's visit), Princess Margaret accompanied by her lady-in-waiting, her private secretary and her personal detective awaited the arrival of their limousine. A little later the King himself appeared and guided the Princess away from her bemused party to his private car. Without further ado, King Hassan drove her round Rabat talking about life. Then, before depositing her at a small palace outside the city, he offered one final piece of advice: 'If your husband is no good, you are quite right to get rid of him!' And with that he bade his dumbfounded guest goodnight and left her in the company of several ladies, of whom one was his mother.

In contrast the Princess's visit to military units based in Cyprus the following November must have seemed a low-key affair.

1977 was written into British history books as the year in which Queen Elizabeth II celebrated the Silver Jubilee of her reign. It was only the second event of its kind this century, for none of the preceding sovereigns except George V had occupied the throne long enough.

The ultimate response to the Jubilee, after earlier widespread indifference, proved phenomenal. On 'Jubilee Day' itself, an estimated one million people packed themselves along the processional route from Buckingham Palace to St Paul's Cathedral, and from the Cathedral to the City Guildhall. It was clear that the monarchy had not enjoyed such a secure position in the affection of the nation for a very long time, despite scornful claims that the celebrating populace had been 'brainwashed'.

On Tuesday 7 June, cold and wet enough to have been mistaken for early autumn, but the day earmarked two years earlier for the official Thanksgiving Service, Princess Margaret rode to St Paul's in an open landau with Lord Linley and Lady Sarah and Princess Alice, Duchess of Gloucester. Also at the Cathedral, though now no more than a face in the congregation was Lord Snowdon. Later, as the Princess left to join other members of the Royal Family at the Guildhall, he collected his son and daughter to take them on to a quiet lunch.

At the start of 1978, a year that was to prove one of the most traumatic of Princess Margaret's entire life, the comparative calm that had existed since her separation from Lord Snowdon was about to be shattered. In its place came renewed speculation about the Princess's friendship with Roddy Llewellyn, who was at the time being launched as a pop singer under the auspices of Claude Wolff and therefore receiving considerable publicity at home and abroad. The Princess had not discouraged Roddy in his plans, for in much the same way that she and her mother had spent many lively evenings singing popular songs around the piano with musical friends such as Noël Coward, so too Princess Margaret and Llewellyn enjoyed singing together.

The publicity about Roddy's new career led to their friendship being highlighted in a series of newspaper articles that were cobbled together from nothing more reliable than old news reports, gossip and innuendo. Taken at face value this speculation was relatively harmless, but it served to focus public attention on a situation already subjected to considerable exaggeration. Such stories might well have been forgotten by the time Princess Margaret flew out to Mustique with friends at the end of February had it not been for a brief but dramatic episode which occurred a few days after their arrival.

On 4 March, Roddy, who had been trying to rid himself of a nagging cold, was suddenly taken seriously ill and was immediately flown to Barbados for emergency treatment. He was admitted to the Diagnostic Clinic, St Michael, from where Dr Richard Haynes announced that he was suffering from an 'upper gastro-intestinal haemorrhage'. A few days later, Princess Margaret arrived on the island, having arranged to stay with Mrs Verna Hull, at Speights-town, St Peter.

To journalists in Fleet Street, news of this kind was a godsend. Royalty was always selling news and if it involved Princess Margaret, so much the better. But when the story broke, anti-monarchist tempers began to boil, and finally erupted almost one week later. By then Roddy had been photographed sitting by his bed, wearing a dressing-gown and a broad smile, and pictures, of the Princess, swimming, walking along a beach and attending 'a lively theatre revue' in Bridgetown, had been wired through to London. She was, said accompanying stories, 'really enjoying life on the sunny isle of Barbados'.

Willie Hamilton leapt to his feet in the House of Commons. In an emotive preamble to his attack on Princess Margaret, he told the House that the Elizabeth Garrett Anderson Hospital for Women in Euston was threatened with closure because lift repairs would cost somewhere between £20,000 and £30,000. 'I suggest taking that £30,000 or whatever it costs from the annuity of the young lady now holidaying in the West Indies,' he said with indignation. Later, in an interview with the press, Hamilton suggested how the Princess might spend her £55,000 Civil List allowance. 'She could set up a dozen play-groups in Scotland,' he said, '£50,000 isn't a big figure, but to the young mothers there, it would be a gold-mine.' He went on, 'If she thumbs her nose at taxpayers by flying off to Mustique ... she shouldn't expect the workers of the country to pay for it.'

Mr Hamilton's tune had not changed, but on this occasion he was joined in duet by Mr Dennis Canavan, the Labour member for West Stirling. Referring to the Princess as a 'parasite' he claimed that, since she did not work, she 'should not get any money at all' – adding that he was going to urge the Chancellor of the Exchequer to stop her annuity because 'her behaviour doesn't merit it'. Canavan was entitled to express his views, but had he looked at the Court Circular, published daily in *The Times* and the *Daily Telegraph*, he may well have had reason to think twice about the Princess not working.

As this latest controversy continued, the *Sunday People* decided to take a dispassionate look at the life and work of the Queen's sister. The newspaper's findings, published on 26 March, revealed that, during the preceding year (1977), the Princess had undertaken at least 126 official engagements excluding overseas duties, formal audiences and occasions when she acted as an official hostess. This figure more than equalled the individual totals of engagements fulfilled by other royal ladies during the same period. Furthermore, the *Sunday People*'s investigation ascertained that during 1976 the Princess had undertaken more engagements in the provinces than any of her female counterparts.

'The Princess', said the report, 'has always provided ammunition for those who say she doesn't help to keep up the royal standard. But the recent, most savage attacks have been of a practical nature. They're concerned with hard cash and value for money.' In winding up its findings, the newspaper had this to say: 'The picture that emerges ... is that while Princess Margaret plays hard, she works hard too.'

This is a fair enough assessment and one which, at this point anyway, did not seem to be tainted by the over-reactions shown elsewhere. Even the clergy decided it was time to enter the fray and the Right Reverend Graham Leonard, Bishop of Truro, said: 'If you accept that you are a public person, you do accept limitations that don't apply to others. I would have thought that the thing that had to be resolved now was in fact how far she can go on being a public person. If you accept the public life, you must accept a severe restriction on your personal conduct.' The Bishop then went on to suggest – as indeed did many others, though less kindly – that the Princess might withdraw from the public arena: 'This I would have thought was a possible way of enabling her to sort out her own affairs.'

Rising above any sentiments of righteous indignation, however, to say nothing of the plentiful – if unsought – advice now being showered upon the Princess, the editor of the *Daily Telegraph*, writing on Thursday 30 March, spoke out cleary and without emotion. It is therefore worth quoting his words at length. Beneath the apposite heading '... Qui mal y pense' one read:

It would be tempting to dismiss the present campaign against Princess Margaret as a nasty combination of envy and prurience plus that residual republican sentiment which is still part of the stock in trade of a section of the British Left. After all, the charges against the Princess are lamentably unspecific: she is said to be doing less than she should to justify the money voted to her by Parliament. But what evidence is there that she refuses or evades public engagements which she ought to fulfil?

Added to this, there is a feeling that what, in the current jargon, is called her 'life-style' does not befit a member of the Royal Family. This complaint is compounded of egalitarian resentment against expensive holidays, high-minded disapproval of 'pop-culture' as exemplified by the pursuits of her friends and a conventional prejudice against close friendships between women and younger men. All these reactions belong to the realm of backbiting gossip, and for that reason are distasteful. No doubt, all societies have moral conventions which they seek to preserve by the pressure of public opinion, but it is more civilized and humane to exert that pressure by praising the virtuous than by hounding those deemed to have erred.

Those who believe in an hereditary monarchy maintain that, as well as its other advantages, that institution will, on the long view, fulfil this representational task more effectively than an elective presidency. They point to the present Queen as the most glittering vindication of that faith. But it is part of the price of an hereditary system of selection that the good must be accepted with the less good. Some forms of personal public behaviour by a Monarch may indeed make it impossible for him to discharge his representational role. Thus, it was held to be impossible for Edward VIII to remain King and supreme Governor of the Church of England while marrying a divorcee. But to expect not only the occupant of the throne but the entire Royal Family to provide a perpetual exemplar of moral and aesthetic perfection is to ask too much, and would be to ask too much even in a society which was far clearer than ours is about what constitutes these ideals.

Noble sentiments as well as undisguised abuse had been expressed now for weeks. And if Princess Margaret had not been informed of the climate of public opinion while she was away in the West Indies, she was certainly made fully conversant with events upon her return. But for one final word on the entire subject, its cause and repercussions, Milton Shulman wrote in the London *Evening Standard* of Friday 7 April:

The present spectacle of churchmen, politicians and headline writers undergoing convulsive spasms of outrage and indignation over Princess Margaret's relationship with Roddy Llewellyn will be viewed by posterity with incredulity.

Princess Margaret still has a useful role to play and she should be allowed to perform it without being harassed by sanctimonious abuse and hypocritical cant.

In a letter to the writer Theo Aronson, Princess Alice, Countess of Athlone, doubtless spoke for the silent majority when she said, 'I do wish they would leave poor Princess Margaret alone.' At this time, as if to prove the point that chills and colds are insufficient reasons for her to cancel engagements, the Princess continued to fulfil her official schedule. By 5 April, however, she had developed flu and as a result she was ordered to bed and forbidden to attend the confirmation of her daughter. The ceremony took place that day in the nave of St George's Chapel, Windsor Castle, with Prince Edward, Lady Helen Windsor and James Ogilvy joining the fourteen-year-old Lady Sarah before the Archbishop of Canterbury, Dr Donald Coggan.

For Princess Margaret, having to miss so important an occasion in her daughter's life caused great sadness, but as an official communiqué explaining the Princess's absence stated, 'Against her personal wishes, but on the strict advice of her doctors, the Princess was prevented from attending the service.' Lord Snowdon was there, however, with Lord Linley (who had been confirmed in St George's Chapel at the same time as Prince Andrew in 1975) and most members of the Royal Family. Afterwards at a celebratory lunch Princess Margaret was allowed to look in for a short time.

Three days later, believing that the worst of her illness had passed, the Princess determined to carry on with her engagements, lest further absence should again give rise to criticism. During the early evening of 8 April, therefore, she drove through unexpected snow to attend a charity concert at Westminster Cathedral, and as her health improved, so she was able to keep each of the functions in her diary. These included a local engagement on 26 April at the Royal Garden Hotel, literally on the corner of the driveway to Kensington Palace. There, as President of Barnardos, the Princess presented the Champion Children of the Year Awards. The presentations were televised during the B.B.C.'s *Nationwide* programme and Princess Margaret looked fitter than she had for some time, reading out the names of the recipients, presenting the prizes and coaxing a few words out of the children who had come to London from every part of the United Kingdom.

A day's engagements in Manchester followed and it was from there that she returned 'feeling like death'. The following morning the Princess's doctor saw her at Kensington Palace and, suspecting not the severe attack of gastro-entiritis claimed by the press, but hepatitis, he took a blood sample. Results of the test confirmed his suspicions and, because the disease is contagious, the Princess was rushed to the King Edward VII Hospital for Officers in Marylebone and kept in isolation.

From Clarence House, Major John Griffin, who acts as press secretary to both Queen Elizabeth the Queen Mother and Princess Margaret, said, 'She has been very much under the weather lately, feeling very ill.' And a friend was quoted as having said that the Princess '... kept going with official engagements although she was not up to it. She is run down and just about exhausted'.

A few months before, as Jubilee year drew to a close, Lord Snowdon – who had been keeping a low profile since the separation – finally moved in to a house in Launceston Place, a quiet street running between Victoria Road and Gloucester Road, on foot no more than ten minutes from Kensington Palace. Princess Margaret has visited the house on only one occasion, and that was after Tony had telephoned to say he wanted to 'talk about something'. It was then that the question of divorce first seriously occurred to the Princess.

Whether the divorce was on Lord Snowdon's mind that day may never be known, but certainly nothing of any significance was discussed during the Princess's visit. It was only on her way out that she decided to open the subject in passing. 'I thought for one moment you were going to ask for a divorce,' she said.

The matter then lay dormant until several weeks later when Snowdon admitted that he would prefer the marriage to be dissolved. He continued to maintain, however, that thoughts of remarrying had not entered his head, much less been allowed to influence his decision. Princess Margaret understood.

By the time this decision came to light publicly on Wednesday 10 May, the pendulum of so-called public opinion had started to swing noticeably in the Princess's favour. And it became even more apparent as later editions of the London *Evening News* and *Evening Standard* that day shared a common banner headline: Margaret A Divorce.

A few hours earlier a statement issued from Kensington Palace had announced:

Her Royal Highness The Princess Margaret, Countess of Snowdon, and the Earl of Snowdon, after two years of separation have agreed that their marriage should formally be ended. Accordingly Her Royal Highness will start the necessary legal proceedings.

That the Princess was suing for the divorce, said her office, was 'a technicality; one party has to start the proceedings. The marriage has broken down and the couple have lived apart for two years. These are obviously the grounds for divorce.' But it was also stated that the Princess and Lord Snowdon would continue to see each other 'on a friendly basis' as they had during the period of their separation.

That evening as Snowdon was leaving his home to attend a Design and Arts Award event in Park Lane, he paused to speak briefly with waiting newsmen. He said simply, 'I hope you will give support and encouragement to Princess Margaret when she comes out of hospital and goes about her duties again.'

For the next three days, the newspapers sang their way through a hastily composed Requiem. And for a moment it was astonishing to recall that barely three months earlier the less reputable of its members had been baiting Princess Margaret with relentless glee. 'Princess whose fairy tale never came true', 'Margaret's velvet-lined prison', 'Farewell to a fairy tale', 'How the years took their toll' and 'Anguish of a Princess who walks alone' were but a few of the bold-type headlines tacked on to lengthy, tear-jerking articles.

Many of the articles spoke of 1955 and the Peter Townsend episode, recognizing the irony that the combined force of Church, Government and Establishment had then ensured that the Princess – had she followed her hopes to marry the divorced Group Captain – would have been divested of everything she valued, but twenty-two years later, in the face of changing attitudes and more relaxed ideas, that same combined force was powerless to prevent the Princess from taking the last step in the marriage she had made.

It is also interesting to note that the Church had little to say on this occasion. Though the process was slow and laboured, it, too, had begun to move with the times. One example of this concerned Holy Communion. In 1955 the Church had threatened that Princess Margaret would be barred from taking the sacrament if she went ahead and married Townsend. In 1978 the Archbishop of Canterbury, Dr Coggan, in common with other clerics with whom she spoke, told the Princess that the Church had been quite wrong in making such intimidating noises.

After the press post-mortem – the marriage that had started amid such promise, and so on – a further subject was raised. On 14 May Ivan Rowan in the *Sunday Telegraph* and David Sinclair in the *Sunday Times* asked whether Princess Margaret had made divorce 'respectable'. In the late 1970s – even where royalty was concerned – it was difficult to believe that many people would still consider divorce carried a stigma and presented social drawbacks. Divorce had by now become an accepted fact of life, and if Princess Margaret could seriously be seen as making divorce respectable, it was only in the same oblique way that her wedding could be claimed to further the marital ideal.

It is true, however, that Princess Margaret did not look forward to becoming a divorcée, any more than she enjoys the status today. Yet while no royal figure so close in line to the throne had been divorced before, it should not be overlooked that the first marriage of the Princess's cousin, the present Earl of Harewood, had been dissolved in 1967, nor that Queen Victoria, one of the greatest advocates of moral propriety, had accepted the annulment of the marriage of her granddaughter, Princess Marie Louise, in 1900, when such an event was certainly considered shameful.

Princess Margaret left the King Edward VII Hospital for Officers on 11 May, eight days after she had been admitted. As she walked slowly to her car, wearing a grey winter coat and a silk headscarf, and accompanied by a uniformed nurse who was to stay with her at Kensington Palace, onlookers were moved by the obvious signs of suffering on her face.

In a brief statement from the hospital it was said that while the Princess had responded well to treatment, she had been advised not to resume public engagements for at least a month. No special diet had been prescribed for her, but since the disease attacks the liver, it was expected that she would be allowed no alcohol for as long as a year.

Following the publication of photographs showing the Princess leaving hospital, her office received a considerable volume of sympathetic messages of goodwill, including those from fellow-sufferers. Between then and 24 May, when notice was given that the Princess's petition had been heard in Court number 44 of the London Divorce Court, her story was allowed to rest. In court Princess

Margaret was represented by her solicitor, Mr Matthew Farrer, and Lord Snowdon by Mr John Humphries. At 10.20 a.m., twenty-eight petitions were put before Judge Roger Willis. Entry number 20 read: 'HRH The Princess Margaret Rose, Countess of Snowdon v Armstrong-Jones A.C.R., Earl of Snowdon'. Minutes later, decree nisi had been pronounced and rubber-stamped in each of the cases. Six weeks afterwards, on 11 July, the Princess was granted a decree absolute.

As Princess Margaret recovered from her illness that summer, arrangements were being finalized for the official visit she was to make to the South Pacific. Her chief function during the tour, which was to begin at the end of September, was to represent the Queen at celebrations marking the granting of independence to the island of Tuvalu. Her programme also included a visit to Fiji from where she was scheduled to fly on to Japan to bestow the Honorary Grand Cross of the Order of St Michael and St George on the Emperor Hirohito's sister-in-law, the Princess Chichibu. From Tokyo the Princess was to pay a private visit, lasting no more than three days, to Los Angeles and she would then holiday at her house on Mustique before paying an official visit to Dominica, returning to London in November.

The long journey of some six thousand miles to the South Pacific Ellice Island, about to adopt a new identity, was undertaken by Princess Margaret and her party in high spirits, but hardly had they arrived than misfortune again overtook the Princess. For the third time in six months she was struck by a severe illness. 'No sooner had I recovered from one than I was knocked down by another,' she recalls.

The first reception of the tour was held in a small, overcrowded room without proper ventilation or air-conditioning, and when the party left to embark in an open cutter for the fifteen-minute ride out to the Royal New Zealand Frigate *Otago*, they were caught in an unexpected tropical shower. When they arrived at the ship, they climbed up a vertical ladder to the deck and made immediately for their quarters, to be met by a dramatic drop in temperature due to an efficient air-conditioning system.

Later that day, as the Princess was dressing for her evening engagement, she asked that her party should be ready to leave the function at 10 p.m., because she was not feeling too well. At the appointed time, after what had been a tiring day, the Princess returned to the *Otago* and, by now, a much needed opportunity to sleep. During the small hours, however, the Princess awoke in a panic and immediately began ringing for her private secretary Lord Napier. 'I shall never know how long the telephone was ringing before I jerked myself awake,' he said later. Then, in no more than a whisper, he heard Princess Margaret say, 'Thank God you've answered. I'm in great pain . . . I can't breath.'

The ship's doctor was immediately alerted and within minutes he was attending to the Princess who with a temperature of 105° had begun to sink into a state of delirium. Viral pneumonia had set in. For everybody concerned the experience was a nightmare; 'I very nearly died,' the Princess recalls. The critical nature of her condition was not, however, fully released to the press.

The following day Lord Napier stood in for Princess Margaret at the island's independence ceremonies and twenty-four hours later, she was considered well enough to board a Hercules tank carrier, in which a bed and medical equipment had been installed, for the flight to the nearest hospital, nine hours away in Sydney. Considerably weakened though she was, the Princess flatly refused to be carried out on a stretcher. 'You will walk in front of me,' she told her private secretary, 'and the doctor will walk behind, and if I collapse, one of you can catch me.'

Nine days later Princess Margaret carried on with the rest of her programme and flew to Japan for her appointment with Princess Chichibu. From Tokyo, Edward Vale of the *Daily Mirror* filed the story of a brief conversation he had had with the Princess, looking, as he put it, 'like the Margaret of old . . .'.

'She spoke about her sorrow at disappointing thousands of people who had hoped to see her,' [in Tuvalu and Fiji] he wrote, and then quoted her as saying, 'You know, I felt quite dreadful that they were let down. But what could I do?' Then, in a classic understatement, she added, 'I wasn't very well.'

In November, the Princess ended the tour, as planned, with her visit to Dominica. It was there, at a reception for newsmen, that one example of press invention came to light. Chatting informally with a handful of journalists, Princess Margaret noticed one man standing nearby. 'Can I have a private word with you?' he asked. The Princess took him unobtrusively aside to hear him confess that he had sent to London a fictitious story, claiming that she had not been happy with the reception she received on her arrival in Dominica. 'But why?' she asked him, 'it was perfectly lovely.' The truth was, he explained, that it had all been so uneventful from his point of view that he felt bound to invent something to satisfy his superiors. He was very sorry, he said, but it was now too late to stop the item from appearing.

Not long after her return to England, Tony told Princess Margaret that he and Lucy Lindsay-Hogg were to be married, but he would not tell her when. In response, the Princess asked Tony to break the news to David and Sarah. On 15 December, in sharp contrast to his first wedding at Westminster Abbey eighteen years before, Lord Snowdon and Mrs Lindsay-Hogg were married quietly at Kensington registry office in the presence of four friends. Seven months later, on Tuesday 17 July 1979, a daughter, Lady Frances Armstrong-Jones, was born to the second Countess of Snowdon.

For the Royal Family the end of the 1970s was marred by a devastating act of violence. On Monday 27 August 1979, Earl Mountbatten of Burma was assassinated while on holiday at Classiebawn Castle in the Irish Republic. He and members of his family were aboard his yacht, *Shadow V*, when it was blown up by a remote-controlled IRA bomb off the coast of County Sligo. Mountbatten, together with his grandson, Nicholas Knatchbull and a young crew-mate, were killed in the blast. His daughter, Lady Brabourne, her husband and their son Timothy (Nicholas's twin) sustained severe injuries but survived, though Lord Brabourne's mother, who was also with them, died of her injuries the following day.

Princess Margaret was on a visit to America in the immediate aftermath of this event and found herself at the centre of ugly demonstrations indirectly linked with the assassination. They stemmed from a remark she is alleged to have made to the Mayor of Chicago, Mrs Jane Byrne. The Princess, as President of the Royal Ballet, was in the United States to help raise funds for the Royal Opera House. New dressing-rooms were needed for dancers and artistes, and in order to provide them, part of the site of the old Covent Garden fruit and vegetable market needed to be redeveloped. The estimated cost of the project amounted to more than £7 million.

In Chicago that October, Mayor Byrne was at a reception in honour of Princess Margaret, during which she expressed her condolences at Mountbatten's death. The Princess responded by saying how touched the Royal Family had been by the messages of sympathy they had received from Irish people. The following day a Chicago gossip-writer, who had not been invited to the reception, announced in his columns that Princess Margaret had called the Irish 'pigs'. Clearly he could not have heard such a remark himself, and even if it is supposed that his information was received at best, second-hand, his informant would have needed to be standing remarkably close to the Princess, since the noise of amplified music and the raised voices of myriad guests made eavesdropping impossible.

It is believed by many people that Princess Margaret's alleged remark was fabrication designed to whip-up sympathy for the Irish cause in the face of what in America is often regarded as British oppression. But whatever lay behind the false report, the effect was immediately damaging. In an unfortunate attempt to ease the tension of the situation, Mayor Byrne said that the Princess may have been talking about Irish 'jigs', a comment that she soon retracted when she realized it had only made matters worse. Lord Napier issued a denial that any unpleasant remark had been made, but this statement fell on deaf ears.

As Princess Margaret moved on to San Francisco there were threats that the Irish population there were to release a thousand pigs in her path and by the time she arrived in Los Angeles the police were claiming to have discovered an IRA plot to kill her.

If, however, Princess Margaret fell briefly from grace over something she did not say in the autumn of 1979, she was to bounce back only three months later, applauded for something she was seen to have achieved. In January 1980 Princess Margaret's return to public favour was occasioned by her marked loss of weight, and for the next year the media was frequently praising her for what it called the Princess's 'new look'.

'People don't like me when I get fat, do they?' the Princess asks. 'But I seem to have been alternately fat or thin on a two years' basis.' In explaining her reversion to a 'look' that was hardly 'new' she says that her current loss of weight started at the time of her last illness: 'I simply could not eat.' Sixteen months later and two stone lighter, newsmen were describing the Princess as 'radiant', 'dazzling', 'svelte' and 'stunning' to mention but a few of the eulogistic adjectives poured on her.

In April, in response to an official invitation, the now 'startlingly slender' Princess Margaret flew out to the Philippines as the guest of President Marcos. Before her arrival his wife, Imelda had told newsmen that she wanted the Princess to enjoy herself after all that she had suffered in terms of ill health and adverse publicity during the recent past. And the Princess did indeed find herself overwhelmed by generosity.

During her stay she was offered the customary gift of emeralds, but declined them because she could not justify accepting such valuable items from a poor nation. Instead she suggested something that was made from local shells and she was duly presented with an ornamental tree in a clam base 'together with some beautiful shells for my collection'. President Marcos, however, was not to be deterred from giving his guest something more and he personally dived for two large pearls, which he then had set in a brooch for her.

Singapore and Malaysia were also included in the itinerary of this particular ASEAN tour and in July another official visit, long since arranged, was made to Canada.

In 1905 Saskatchewan and Alberta were inaugurated as Canadian provinces, and these provinces were now celebrating the seventy-fifth anniversary of their entry into the Canadian Confederation. Two years earlier the Queen's visit to Saskatchewan had been centred on the capital, Regina, and now in 1980 Princess Margaret, as the Queen's representative, was to take in the northern communities. From Ottawa she flew to Saskatoon, the second largest city in Saskatchewan. From there she travelled to Prince Albert, a region of agricultural industries and railways; toured the Muskoday Indian Reservation and visited the French-speaking community at Zenon Park. A tour of North Battleford took the Princess to the barrack buildings which had seen the North West Rebellion of 1885.

Princess Margaret then flew into Alberta, where she attended a race meeting at the Northlands Racecourse, watching, appropriately, the running of the Princess Margaret Stakes. That evening she was the guest of honour at a western-style barbecue, planned to recapture the days of the goldrush. Entering into the spirit of the occasion, the Princess wore a long, flounced dress of pink lace and an ostrich plume in her hair; completing the outfit with a parasol and mittens.

The only blot on the Princess's otherwise successful official visit was an article by the editor of the *Toronto Sun*. In part, the leader of 23 July read: 'There is something ludicrously hypocritical and in exquisite bad taste about the state visit of Princess Margaret to Canada. She is out West being given the top hat and curtsy treatment as if she were something special rather than a Royal Baggage who has, by her lifestyle, forfeited all right to respect and homage.'

Such empty invective was hardly likely to cause a diplomatic incident, but it did offend Canadians, a large number of whom strongly condemned the article itself as being 'in exquisite bad taste'. There was an outcry from London too, led by the *Sun* and the *Daily Mirror*, which strongly denounced this 'vitriolic attack', while reminding the offending editor that Princess Margaret was not visiting Canada because she was at a loss for something better to do at home.

She was back in England for August and the celebrations of both her mother's and her own birthdays, which this year held particular significance. On the fourth, Queen Elizabeth the Queen Mother was eighty and on the twenty-first the Princess was fifty.

The previous month, on 15 July, a national tribute had been paid to the Queen Mother in the form of a Service of Thanksgiving at St Paul's Cathedral. Like the Queen's Silver Jubilee three years earlier, the ceremony – a state occasion – was surrounded by all the pomp and splendour synonymous with such events. Much more intimate was the scene at the Queen Mother's home on 4 August. It has become a tradition for the Queen Mother to greet the crowd which faithfully assembles outside Clarence House on her birthday, and on this special occasion there were many well-wishers waiting to see her. They were treated to a royal bonus, for several members of her family were also at Clarence House that day, and the Queen and Princess Margaret helped receive the flowers and gifts which people had brought.

Princess Margaret's birthday fell, as always, during the Royal Family's annual summer holiday at Balmoral Castle. To mark the occasion, photographs which had been taken some eight weeks earlier by Norman Parkinson were released.

Two days later the *Daily Telegraph* in its editorial leader paid warm tribute to the Princess, one which gave her particular satisfaction. It read:

> As Princess Margaret this week celebrated her fiftieth birthday in the privacy of her own family, one gossip-columnist opined 'A time when her popularity is at a low ebb'. Now this is an interesting judgement, the more so since this very same gossip-columnist has done more than most to reveal the innermost details of Princess Margaret's private life. If these details have served to make her unpopular to the British people, though he of course does not so argue, it is pretty clear where some of the responsibility for this lies. No doubt we are all guilty of a little hypocrisy here. It is commonly accepted that much of the great popularity of the present Royal Family is attributable to its public manifestation of a family bliss and unity to which we all aspire. It is useless to deny that in this respect Princess Margaret has been the least fortunate of all the living generations of royalty, and perhaps one consequence of this is that she has been punished for failing to live up to the obligingly blissful mirror-image which we expect of our royalty. Yet if she has been so punished by elements in the press, what has been the reaction of the people? There is, in fact, no evidence whatsoever to support the contention that Princess Margaret is unpopular. On the contrary, her tireless public work and appearances, so few of which can, in the nature of things, be reported would rather argue that she richly deserves to win a place in the affections of a fair-minded people, and the British people do have a reputation for being more tolerant and less judgemental, more understanding and less liable to confuse public works with private morals than many of their establishment leaders, sages and scribes. Such a people would surely have privately wished Princess Margaret a very happy fiftieth birthday and more years of greater happiness.

Princess Margaret did not, however, celebrate her birthday until 4 November, the day after her son David, who had by this time left the coeducational school Bedales in Hampshire to attend the John Makepiece School for Craftsmen at Parnham in Dorset, celebrated his twentieth birthday. The ball in honour of the Princess's birthday was held at the Ritz in Piccadilly; organized by fifteen of her friends, it was 'the bash of the year' as one of her relations is alleged to have described it. After a private dinner, attended by nearly every member of the Royal Family, the ball got under way and lasted until the small hours of the next morning when the two hundred guests finally dispersed.

POSTSCRIPT

The weddings of family and friends were prominent features of Princess Margaret's diary during the summer and autumn months of 1981. Chief among them was the marriage of the Prince of Wales and Lady Diana Spencer, which was celebrated at St Paul's Cathedral on 29 July. The Princess's daughter Sarah had been asked to act as chief bridesmaid, an invitation that gave the Princess particular pleasure because of her affection for the bride.

The week of the wedding was a particularly busy time for the members of the Royal Family, who were all involved in entertaining the official guests. Princess Margaret, for her part, gave a luncheon party for twenty-five in the Garden Room at Kensington Palace in honour of Mrs Nancy Reagan, who was representing the President of the United States. On the day of the wedding itself the first carriage procession to St Paul's was led by a semi-State landau containing Princess Margaret and Princess Anne with Lord Linley and Captain Mark Phillips. After the wedding and the departure on honeymoon of the Prince and Princess of Wales, most members of the Royal Family attended a private party that evening at Claridges Hotel arranged by the Earl of Lichfield's sister, Lady Elizabeth Anson, where they were able to dissipate any feelings of anti-climax.

A week before the royal wedding one of the Princess's ladies-in-waiting, the Honourable Davina Woodhouse, had married Earl Alexander of Tunis and in October, Elizabeth Paget, who had succeeded Davina as permanent lady-in-waiting, was married to Dr Angus Blair, a Harley Street specialist. But the most unexpected engagement to some was undoubtedly that of Roddy Llewellyn, who had by now been close to Princess Margaret for almost eight years.

Although Roddy had sometimes said he was too selfish for marriage, he had now made up his mind that this was what he wanted. His bride-to-be was Tatiana Soskin, a fashion designer who was erroneously described by the press as a travel writer, even an heiress. The daughter of a Russian, the late Paul Soskin, and his wife Minora (now Mrs Victor Simaika), Tania, as she is better known, had been a friend of Roddy's for ten years, but it was only towards the end of 1980 that they began going out together and that was when Princess Margaret first talked to Roddy about his intentions. If the Princess was at all upset when she learned of his engagement a few months later, she did not show it. Nor did it affect the continuing warmth of their friendship. Indeed she told him, when he asked, that she would be delighted to attend the wedding.

Originally the ceremony was to have taken place in the small church at Llanvair on 27 June, a date that fitted in with Princess Margaret's activities, but arranging a wedding in Wales proved more difficult than envisaged and plans had to be changed in favour of a new date and a different location. Thus, Saturday 11 July 1981 at Marlow in Buckinghamshire, where Tania's uncle has a house, was finally settled upon.

That day an estimated crowd of some eight hundred, including press and television cameramen, gathered outside the parish church of All Saints, at Marlow Bridge, waiting to take a look at Roddy and his bride. Some were said to be waiting for a glimpse of Princess Margaret, but if so they waited in vain. For five days earlier, on 6 July, the Princess accompanied for the first time by seventeen-year-old Sarah (who was studying A-level art at Bedales) had left London at the start of yet another official visit to Canada.

On this occasion the visit was being made in connexion with the fiftieth anniversary celebrations of the Royal Ballet. While there, the Princess chose to vary her schedule to visit a silver-mine at Kid Creek, five hundred miles north of Toronto, in preference to attending a performance at the Shakespeare Festival at Stratford, Ontario. Arriving at the pit-head amid the cheers of several hundred miners, mother and daughter climbed into red overalls and white safety helmets before being lowered 1600 feet down the main shaft of the mine.

From Canada Princess Margaret and Lady Sarah were to have travelled on to Washington, but in the wake of pro-IRA demonstrations staged in New York during Prince Charles's visit a month before, it had been decided that the visit should be cancelled.

Three months later, duty took Princess Margaret abroad once more. On this occasion, as the Queen's personal representative, she flew out to Swaziland where King Sobhuza II was celebrating the Diamond Jubilee of his reign. The high spot of the week's festivities was the ceremony of Trooping the Colour – Sobhuza-style. The King's regiment having been trained by British Army Officers, was drilled to advance, troop and retreat in an African version of the Sovereign's Birthday Parade observed in London each summer. The only difficulty with the African version was that it lasted five hours without a break, rather than the two hours which Princess Margaret and her party were expecting, and it was only at the ceremony's close that the Princess was able to invest the King with the Order of St Michael and St George; slipping the riband over his head-dress and fastening the star to his necklet, his only garment save an ancient leopard-skin skirt.

In all Princess Margaret undertook five official visits abroad during 1981. In January she had undertaken engagements in snowbound Athens and later visited Munich. After Canada and Swaziland came Antigua, where the Princess attended ceremonies marking the island's independence, before going on briefly to St Vincent.

Her private life was again a matter of press speculation. In spring, the traditional time for romance, stories appeared on the front of one or two national newspapers that Princess Margaret was planning to remarry. This idle speculation almost became read as fact when the *Sun*, on 22 April 1982, declared in bold type: 'Margaret All Set to Wed'. The Princess, said the newspaper's columnist, was about to marry 'a wealthy widower' with whom she had fallen 'deeply in love'.

That she was in love with anybody – deeply or otherwise – was news to the Princess herself. It was also news to Norman Lonsdale, the fifty-four-year-old businessman (whom Princess Margaret has known for very many years) named as her husband-to-be.

'I have never proposed marriage to Princess Margaret,' he said 'and I am not likely to do so in the forseeable future.' He went on to say, 'I have a great deal of respect for her. I think she has an extremely good brain, she knows a great deal about the theatre, ballet and that sort of thing. She is extremely stimulating to be with ... a very outspoken person ... what she has to say is usually right.'

What she had to say about these latest stories was also outspoken. 'Absolute rubbish!' was her comment. For a change, the news reports had not originated in Fleet Street but in Glasgow, where the Princess had opened a new hotel. On that occasion, it was noticed that she was wearing a ring on the third finger of her left hand. Scottish newsmen put two and two together, came up with five, and pronounced the ring to be a token of an engagement.

'When a fifty-one-year-old woman ... puts a twenty-five-year-old ring on her finger [in this case it was a cabachon star-sapphire], it does not mean she is going to get married,' the Princess responded. To the more observant the engagement story caused no more than a raised eyebrow, for ever since her betrothal was announced in February 1960, Princess Margaret had never been seen without a ring of one description or another on that finger.

Nonetheless, it was almost inevitable that stories of remarriage would be widely mooted at some stage, even though Princess Margaret herself could not be more adamant that she has no intention of marrying again. Notwithstanding the strength of her feelings on the matter, however, it is only fair to say that it has always been considered a lady's prerogative to change her mind.

What then of Princess Margaret's future? Clearly her life will continue to be influenced by the part she plays in the official functions of the Royal Family. And it is not unreasonable to suppose that she will be able to devote yet more energy to the organizations she is most interested in. By then the younger generation, headed by the Prince and Princess of Wales, Princess Anne, Prince Andrew and Prince Edward, will have become even more prominent members of what was once called the 'Royal Road Show'. Indeed, a new Royal Family has already begun to emerge from the midst of the present one.

More personally, however, the Princess – as is clear to those who know her – has regained much of the vitality for which she was once justly famous. The past, as she is the first to admit, has left its mark, but while the emotional scars remain, her memories are now less painful. 'Even during the bad times in her life, and they were hell,' says one of her friends, 'she never gave up hope ... It was probably very much a case of the royal stiff upper lip.'

Yet while the minority that has never failed to come down heavily on her will doubtless reserve the right to continue to do so, some of its ranks have at last recognized that enough is enough. 'Battered by life, but still a winner,' one journalist recently wrote. 'In different times her life could have been a fairy tale. Yet she has learned to be a survivor.' Princess Margaret would not argue with that. But nor could anybody deny that this Princess has endured more than her fair share of calumny and has come through it all with great dignity.

APPENDIX I

THE CIVIL LIST

The origins of the Civil List go back more than two hundred years, to 1760, when King George III upon his accession to the throne surrendered the revenues from the Crown Lands to Parliament in return for an annual income: the Civil List. A similar surrender has been made by all successive sovereigns, but it has only been since 1975 that the Civil List allocation has been automatically increased each year to keep abreast of inflation.

Under the terms of the Civil List the sovereign and several – but by no means all – members of the Royal Family receive direct incomes from the Treasury. Such annuities are not salaries in the usual sense: monies are not transferred direct from the Treasury to the personal bank accounts of members of the Royal Family for them to use for private purposes. Civil List incomes are made specifically to reimburse the Queen, Queen Elizabeth the Queen Mother, Princess Margaret and other members of the Royal Family for their *official* expenditure, that is to say funds are provided annually to cover the cost of their *official* lives.

During 1982 the Treasury distributed total Civil List allowances of £4,612,883. From that sum the Queen – in keeping with a practice established a few years ago – refunded to the Treasury the sum of £304,700. This figure represents allowances allocated to certain junior members of the Royal Family (the Duke of Gloucester, Princess Alice, Duchess of Gloucester, the Duke of Kent and Princess Alexandra, the Hon. Mrs Angus Ogilvy). The Queen, however, covers these outgoings personally, and the grant is therefore returned to the Treasury. In effect, this means that the total Civil List allocation during 1982 amounted to £4,308,183.

For the year 1981–82 the Treasury was in direct receipt of £14 million from the Crown Estates. From this it will be appreciated how much, in terms of hard cash, the monarchy contributes to the Exchequer.

THE HOUSEHOLD OF HRH THE PRINCESS MARGARET

In the 1982 Civil List increases, Princess Margaret's allowance was raised from £98,000 to £104,500, a sum which may initially seem large but which has to cover the considerable costs involved in carrying out royal duties. The major item of expenditure is staff salaries; in the Princess's own words, 'To do this job properly, one needs competent staff and they have to be paid.'

In all, Princess Margaret employs a staff of ten, divided into Household and Domestic. Those in the former category are the Princess's Private Secretary, Major the Lord Napier & Ettrick; her Personal Secretary, Miss Muriel Murray Brown, and their secretary Miss Charlotte Drummond. In the latter category are the Princess's butler, housekeeper, personal dresser, chef, chauffeur, and two part-time domestics. All are paid salaries by Princess Margaret linked to those of the Civil Service. Such payments are made from Her Royal Highness's Civil List income.

From the same fund are covered heating and lighting costs for the Princess's official residence, number 1A Clock Court, together with rates, which currently amount to some £10,000. Princess Margaret is similarly responsible for the rates, heating and lighting for the two cottages and three flats that are occupied, rent free, by members of her staff.

Running and maintaining official transport, in this case the Rolls-Royce which the Princess bought from private funds, is also allowable as part of the total expenditure for official travelling. During 1981 Princess Margaret fulfilled 188 official engagements: 101 in Britain and 87 abroad. The Princess also gave eleven formal audiences to people such as retiring senior officers.

Essentially Princess Margaret's Household might best be described as a business concern, trading primarily in public relations. When viewed in this way, it is easy to understand the costs that are necessarily incurred. Indeed, for every example of official royal expenditure, a comparable outgoing may be found in a commercial outfit of similar size. In both cases business premises and staff are paid for, and so too are the services of accountants. (The Princess in fact engages an accountant on a part-time basis.) Other considerations include the cost of purchase, hire and maintenance of office equipment, telephone, postage and stationary – which together represent a very considerable outgoing – plus such items as provisions and household supplies.

When such expenditure is totalled at the end of each financial year, it is not difficult to justify the need for the Princess's Civil List annuity. Nor does it require a great deal of imagination to understand why, in the recent past, Princess Margaret has been obliged to supplement her household's expenses from relatively modest private funds.

THE PRESIDENCIES, PATRONAGES AND SERVICE APPOINTMENTS OF HRH THE PRINCESS MARGARET

PRESIDENCIES

Chorleywood College for Girls with Little or No Sight

Dockland Settlements

Barnardo's

The English Folk Dance and Song Society

Friends of the Elderly and Gentlefolk's Help

The Girl Guides Association

The Horder Centre for Arthritics

The League of Pity

National Society for the Prevention of Cruelty to Children

The Royal Ballet

Royal Scottish Society for Prevention of Cruelty to Children

Sadler's Wells Foundation

Scottish Children's League

The Sunshine Homes and Schools for Blind Children

The Victoria League

Grand President of the St John Ambulance Association and Brigade

Joint President of the Lowland Brigade Club

President and Chairman of Council, The Invalid Children's Aid Association

PATRONAGES

The Architects' Benevolent Society

The Barristers' Benevolent Association

Bristol Royal Workshops for the Blind

British Sailors' Society Ladies' Guild

Coventry Cathedral Ten-year Development Plan

Friends of St John's (Smith Square)

Friends of Southwark Cathedral

The Light Infantry Club

Linked Cities Congress (Great Britain and North Rhine-Westphalia)

The London Festival Ballet

The Mary Hare Grammar School for the Deaf

The Mathilda and Terence Kennedy Institute of Rheumatology

The Migraine Trust

The National Pony Society

The Pottery and Glass Trades' Benevolent Institution

The Princess Margaret Hospital and Lodge (Canadian Cancer Society Auxiliary)

The Princess Margaret Rose Hospital, Edinburgh

Queen Alexandra's Royal Army Nursing Corps Association

Royal College of Nursing and National Council of Nurses of the United Kingdom

St Margaret's Chapel Guild, Edinburgh Castle

St Pancras Housing Association in Camden

Services Kinema Corporation

Heart Disease and Diabetes Research Trust

The Cambridge Festival Association

Scottish Association of Youth Clubs

Scottish Community Drama Association

Suffolk Regimental Association

Tenovus (Institute for Cancer Research)

Union of Schools for Social Service (The Peckham Settlement)

University of London Choir

The West Indies Olympic Association

The Zebra Trust

Patron-in-Chief of the English Harbour Repair Fund

Honorary Patron of the Winnipeg Art Gallery

Vice-Patron of the Royal Anglian Regimental Association

(Temporary) Patron of:
  The Commonwealth Countries' League
  The Institute of Home Help Organisers
  The Royal Caledonian Ball

Freedom of The City of London

Freeman of The Worshipful Company of Haberdashers

Freedom of The Royal Burgh of Queensferry

Honorary Air Commodore of Royal Air Force, Coningsby

Honorary Doctor of Music, University of London

Honorary Doctor of Law, University of Cambridge

Honorary Doctor of Laws, University of British Columbia

Honorary Doctor of Letters, University of Keele

Master of The Bench, the Honourable Society of Lincoln's Inn

Honorary Fellow of The Royal Institute of British Architects

Honorary Fellow of The Royal Society of Medicine

Honorary Fellow of The Royal College of Surgeons of England

Honorary Fellow of The Royal
College of Obstetricians and
Gynaecologists

Honorary Fellow of Honorary Life
Fellow of The Zoological
Society of London

Chancellor of the University of
Keele

Service Appointments

Colonel-in-Chief of 15th/19th The
King's Royal Hussars

Colonel-in-Chief of Royal
Highland Fusiliers (Princess
Margaret's Own Glasgow and
Ayrshire Regiment)

Colonel-in-Chief of Queen
Alexandra's Royal Army
Nursing Corps

Colonel-in-Chief of Highland
Fusiliers of Canada (Militia)

Colonel-in-Chief of Women's
Royal Australian Army Corps

Deputy Colonel-in-Chief of The
Royal Anglian Regiment

Decorations

Grand Cross of the Royal
Victorian Order

Imperial Order of the Crown of
India

Dame Grand Cross of the Order of
St John of Jerusalem

Grand Cross of the Order of the
Lion of The Netherlands

Order of the Brilliant Star of
Zanzibar, 1st Class

Grand Cross of the Order of the
Crown of Belgium

Order of the Crown, Lion and
Spears of Toro Kingdom,
Uganda

Order of the Precious Crown, 1st
Class, Japan

Grand Cross (1st Class) of the
Order of Merit of the Federal
Republic of Germany

Official Overseas Visits 1947–82

1947	South Africa
1948	The Netherlands
1949	Italy, Switzerland and France
1950	Malta and Tripoli
1951	France
1953	Norway
	Southern Rhodesia
1954	Federal Republic of Germany
1955	West Indies
1956	Sweden
	East Africa and Indian Ocean Dependencies
1958	Federal Republic of Germany
	West Indies
	Canada
	Belgium
1959	Portugal
1960	Belgium
1961	Norway
1962	Jamaica
1963	Federal Republic of Germany (Münster)
	Federal Republic of Germany (Westphalia and Brüggen)
1964	Denmark
1965	Uganda
	Netherlands
	The United States of America
1966	Hong Kong
	France
1967	Belgium
1968	The United States of America
	France
1969	Japan
	Cambodia
	Thailand
	Iran
1970	Yugoslavia
1971	France
	Canada
1972	British Virgin Islands
	Italy
	Federal Republic of Germany

Seychelles
Western Australia
Singapore
1973 Barbados
Federal Republic of
Germany
1974 Cyprus
The United States of
America
Canada
1975 Federal Republic of
Germany
Australia
Bermuda
1976 Morocco
Tunisia
Cyprus
1977 Italy
The United States of
America

1978 Tuvalu
Japan
Dominica
1979 The United States of
America
1980 Federal Republic of
Germany
The Philippines
Singapore
Malaysia
Canada
1981 Greece
Federal Republic of
Germany
Canada
Swaziland
Antigua
St Vincent
1982 Federal Republic of
Germany
Italy

OUTLINE ITINERARY OF THE 1965 VISIT TO THE UNITED STATES OF AMERICA AND BERMUDA

THURSDAY 4 NOVEMBER

1 a.m. Princess Margaret and Lord Snowdon leave London Airport on BOAC's Flight Number BA 501.

1.35 p.m. Arrive J. F. Kennedy International Airport, New York. Presentations.

2.50 p.m. Take off on BOAC's Flight number BA 583.

6.05 p.m. Arrive at San Francisco International Airport. Presentations.

6.15 p.m. Leave San Francisco Airport.

6.45 p.m. Arrive Press Club for meeting with the Press (the Princess will make a speech or statement).

7.10 p.m. Leave the Press Club.

7.15 p.m. Arrive Huntington Hotel.

FRIDAY 5 NOVEMBER

10.45 a.m. Leave Huntington Hotel.
Arrive City Hall, San Francisco. Received by the Mayor. Presentations.

11.15 a.m. Leave City Hall.

11.30 a.m. Return to Huntington Hotel.

11.50 a.m. Leave Huntington Hotel.

12 noon Arrive at Hilton Hotel for Charity Luncheon arranged by the English-Speaking Union and display of British fashions by I. Magnin & Co.

2.40 p.m. Leave Hilton Hotel.

Afternoon Possible sight-seeing trip.

6 p.m. Leave Huntington Hotel.

6.15 p.m. Arrive at 2516 Pacific Avenue for Reception by H.M. Consul-General.

7 p.m.   Leave Consul-General's Reception.

SATURDAY 6 NOVEMBER

9.30 a.m.   Leave Huntington Hotel.

9.45 a.m.   Board Hovercraft.

10.10 a.m.   Arrive Oakland Airport.
Presentations.
Depart from Oakland.

10.40 a.m.   Arrive at the University of California, Berkeley.
Visit to Cyclotron.

11.35 a.m.   Leave University of California.

12 noon   Take off from Oakland Airport for visit to Monterey.

SUNDAY 7 NOVEMBER

9.55 a.m.   Leave Huntington Hotel on foot.

10 a.m.   Arrive at Grace Cathedral for Matins.
Return to Huntington Hotel.

12.15 p.m.   Leave Huntington Hotel.

12.45 p.m.   Take off from San Francisco International Airport in an Andover of the Queen's Flight.

2.30 p.m.   Arrive at Los Angeles International Airport.
Presentations.
Meeting with the Press (speech).

3 p.m.   Leave Los Angeles Airport.

3.30 p.m.   Arrive at Beverly Hills Hotel.

Afternoon   Visit to the home of Mr Vincent Price to see his art

collection followed by visit to the home of Mr S. Brody.

MONDAY 8 NOVEMBER

10 a.m.   Leave Beverly Hills Hotel.

10.10 a.m.   Arrive at the J. W. Robinson, Beverly Hills store, to see a display of British goods.

10.30 a.m.   Leave the store.

10.45 a.m.   Arrive at Los Angeles County Museum of Art.

11.30 a.m.   Leave the Museum.

12.15 p.m.   Arrive at Universal Studios, North Hollywood.
Presentations and Drinks.

12.45 p.m.   Luncheon with representatives of all major film studios.

Afternoon   Watch filming.

5.15 p.m.   Return to Beverly Hills Hotel.

7.30 p.m.   Leave the Beverly Hills Hotel.

8 p.m.   Arrive at the Hollywood Palladium for the World Adoption International Fund Ball.
Dinner.
British Fashion Show organised by I. Magnin & Co.

Later   Return to Hotel.

TUESDAY 9 NOVEMBER

10.30 a.m.   Princess Margaret leaves Beverly Hills Hotel.

10.30 a.m.   Lord Snowdon leaves Beverly Hills Hotel.

11.15 a.m.   Her Royal Highness arrives at the British Home organized by the Daughters of the British Empire.

Presentations.
Tour of Home.

11.15 a.m. Lord Snowdon
arrives at Johnson Motors Inc. at
Duarte.
Presentations and laying of
foundation stone by Lord
Snowdon.

11.40 a.m. Her Royal Highness
leaves the British Home.

11.40 a.m. Lord Snowdon leaves
Johnson Motors Inc.

11.55 a.m. Lord Snowdon
arrives at the California Institute
of Technology.

12 noon Her Royal Highness
arrives at the Institute.
Presentations and drinks.
Luncheon.
Tour of Campus and
laboratories.
Drive to Auditorium Building
for Jet Propulsion Laboratory.

3 p.m. Leave the California
Institute of Technology.

3.45 p.m. Return to Beverly
Hills Hotel.

Afternoon Lord Snowdon has
private meeting with architects
at the office of Mr Welton
Becket.

6.15 p.m. Leave the Beverly
Hills Hotel.

6.45 p.m. Arrive at 450 South
June Street, for Reception given
by H.M. Consul-General.

7.30 p.m. Leave the Consul-
General's Reception.

WEDNESDAY 10 NOVEMBER

10.45 a.m. Leave Beverly Hills
Hotel.

11.15 a.m. Arrive at Music
Centre for private visit.

11.45 a.m. Leave Music Centre.

12 noon Arrive at Los Angeles
City Hall.
Received by the Mayor.
Presentations.

12.20 p.m. Leave the City Hall.

1 p.m. Arrive at Los Angeles
International Airport.

1.10 p.m. Leave Los Angeles in
an Andover of The Queen's
Flight.

4.30 p.m. Arrive at Tucson,
Arizona.
Received by The Honourable
Lewis and Mrs Douglas.

6 p.m. Arrive at Country Club
for Cocktail Party given by Mr
and Mrs Douglas. Guests include
the Governor of Arizona and
the Mayor of Tucson.

THURSDAY 11 NOVEMBER–SUNDAY
14 NOVEMBER

Private long weekend.

MONDAY 15 NOVEMBER

10.15 a.m. Leave Tucson,
Arizona, in a Jet Star of the
President's Flight.

5 p.m. Princess Margaret and
Lord Snowdon arrive at
Andrews Air Force Base,
Washington, on a Jet Star of the
President's Flight.
Presentations.

5.10 p.m. Leave the Air Force
Base.

5.45 p.m. Arrive at the British
Embassy (H.M.'s Ambassador's
residence).

6.30 p.m. Leave the Residence.

6.45 p.m. Arrive at the Statler
Hilton Hotel for Press
Reception given jointly by the
Woman's National Press Club
and the National Press Club.
(Her Royal Highness will make
a speech or statement).

7.30 p.m. Leave the Statler
Hilton Hotel.

7.45 p.m. Return to Residence.

8 p.m. Dine at the British
Residence.

TUESDAY 16 NOVEMBER

9.45 a.m. Leave the British
Residence.

10 a.m. Arrive at Arlington
Cemetery to lay wreath on
President Kennedy's grave.

10.15 a.m. Leave Arlington
Cemetery.

10.55 a.m. Arrive at Mount
Vernon.
Presentations.
Tour of house and gardens.

11.40 a.m. Leave Mount
Vernon.
Visit Jefferson Memorial, the
Capitol, the Washington
Monument and the Lincoln
Memorial.

1 p.m. Return to Residence.

1.15 p.m. Official Luncheon at
Residence.

3.25 p.m. Leave the Residence.

3.30 p.m. Arrive at Washington
Cathedral.
Tour of Cathedral.

4 p.m. Leave the Cathedral.

4.15 p.m. Arrive at 3147 P.

Street N.W., for a visit to Mrs
Charles F. Willis.

5. p.m. Leave Mrs Willis's house.
house.

5.15 p.m. Return to Residence.

6 p.m. Attend H.M.
Ambassador's Reception at
Residence.

6.50 p.m. Leave the Reception.

7.55 p.m. Leave the Residence.

8 p.m. Arrive at the home of
Admiral Sir Nigel Henderson,
Head of the British Defence
Staff, for a dinner party.

Later Attend a party given by
Mrs Katzenbach, wife of the
Attorney-General.

WEDNESDAY 17 NOVEMBER

9.50 a.m. Leave the Residence.

10 a.m. Arrive at the Sharpe
Health School, 4300 Thirteenth
Street, NW.
Tour the School.

10.45 a.m. Leave the Sharpe
Health School.

11 a.m. Arrive at Bryce Park,
Massachusetts Avenue.
Dedication of the Park (and
speech) by Her Royal Highness.

11.20 a.m. Leave Bryce Park and
return to Residence.

11.35 a.m. Leave the Residence.

11.50 a.m. Arrive at Dunbarton
Oaks, to tour house and
museum.

12.20 p.m. Leave Dunbarton
Oaks.

12.30 p.m. Return to the
Residence.

1 p.m. Official luncheon at the
Residence.

3 p.m.   Visit National Gallery of Art.

3.55 p.m.   Leave the National Gallery of Art.

4.05 p.m.   Her Royal Highness arrives at the home of Mrs Edward Kennedy to meet the wives of Senators.
Lord Snowdon will visit the Washington Zoo.

4.45 p.m.   Her Royal Highness will leave Mrs Kennedy's house.

5 p.m.   Return to the Residence.

7.40 p.m.   Leave the Residence.

7.50 p.m.   Arrive at the White House.
Greeted by the President and Mrs Johnson.
Dinner.

THURSDAY 18 NOVEMBER

10.30 a.m.   Leave the Residence.

10.45 a.m.   Arrive at the Smithsonian Institute.
Tour.

11.30 a.m.   Leave the Smithsonian.

11.45 a.m.   Return to the Residence.

12 noon   Tree-planting ceremony in the Embassy grounds.

1.15 p.m.   Luncheon at the Residence.

2.25 p.m.   Leave the Residence.

3.15 p.m.   Take off from Andrews Air Force Base in an Andover of The Queen's Flight.

4.30 p.m.   Arrive at La Guardia Airport, New York.
Presentations.

4.40 p.m.   Leave the Airport.

5.25 p.m.   Arrive at the Waldorf-Astoria Hotel for Meeting with the Press. (Her Royal Highness will make a speech or statement).

5.45 p.m.   Leave the Waldorf-Astoria Hotel.

6 p.m.   Arrive at 163 East 63rd Street, the home of Mr and Mrs John Hay Whitney.

FRIDAY 19 NOVEMBER

11.45 a.m.   Leave East 63rd Street.

11.55 a.m.   Arrive at Empire State Building.

12.25 p.m.   Leave.

12.30 p.m.   Arrive at United Nations Headquarters.
Presentations.
Luncheon.
Tour.
Visit a Working Session.

3.20 p.m.   Leave United Nations Headquarters.

3.30 p.m.   Arrive at 845 Third Avenue.
Visit British Consulate-General Offices.
Visit Offices of U.K. Mission to the United Nations.
Visit British Information Services Offices.

4.15 p.m.   Princess Margaret leaves 845 Third Avenue and walks across the road to the Headquarters of the Girl Scouts of the United States. Tour.

4.15 p.m.   Lord Snowdon leaves the United Nations and returns to 163 East 63rd Street.

4.30 p.m.   Her Royal Highness leaves the Girl Scouts H.Q.

4.45 p.m. Her Royal Highness returns to East 63rd Street.

4.55 p.m. Lord Snowdon leaves East 63rd Street.

5.15 p.m. Lord Snowdon arrives at 51st Street for private cocktail party given by Time–Life.

8 p.m. Her Royal Highness and Lord Snowdon arrive at the Waldorf-Astoria Hotel for a Ball given by the English-Speaking Union of the United States, the Pilgrims of the United States and the U.S. Churchill Foundation.

SATURDAY 20 NOVEMBER

11.15 a.m. Leave East 63rd Street.

11.30 a.m. Arrive at the Metropolitan Museum of Art. Tour.

12.30 p.m. Leave the Museum.

12.45 p.m. Arrive at the Museum of Modern Art. Luncheon. Tour.

3 p.m. Leave Museum of Modern Art.

3.30 p.m. Arrive at the Police Athletic League at Mulberry Street.

3.45 p.m. Leave Mulberry Street.

3.55 p.m. Board launch for trip on Hudson River.

4.25 p.m. Land at Yacht Basin in West 70s.

4.45 p.m. Arrive at 163 East 63rd Street.

5.15 p.m. Lord Snowdon arrives at the Seagram Building, to meet young architects at Mr

Philip Tomlinson's office.

5.30 p.m. Princess Margaret leaves East 63rd Street.

6 p.m. Princess Margaret arrives arrives at 110 Street to visit the New York Cathedral and unveils a window.

6.30 p.m. Her Royal Highness leaves the Cathedral.

7 p.m. Her Royal Highness returns to East 63rd Street. Lord Snowdon arrives at East 63rd Street.

8.30 p.m. Princess Margaret and Lord Snowdon leave East 63rd Street.

8.45 p.m. Arrive at East 52nd Street for a party given by Mr Joshua Logan.

SUNDAY 21 NOVEMBER

Private engagements.

MONDAY 22 NOVEMBER

10.30 a.m. Princess Margaret and Lord Snowdon drive along Fifth Avenue and visit shops with British displays.

11.30 a.m. Princess Margaret will arrive at the Biltmore Hotel to open the Annual Bazaar (The British Fair) of the Daughters of the British Empire and will make a speech. Lord Snowdon will visit more shops in Fifth Avenue.

12 noon Her Royal Highness will leave the Biltmore Hotel.

12.10 p.m. Lord Snowdon arrives at 41 East 57th Street.

12.15 p.m. Her Royal Highness will arrive at 41 East 57th Street to open the British Painters Exhibition at the Marlborough–Gerson Gallery.

12.45 p.m.   Leave the Gallery.

1.15 p.m.   Arrive at the Chase Manhattan Bank for a Wall Street luncheon given by Mr David Rockefeller.

3 p.m.   Leave the Chase Manhattan Bank.

3.15 p.m.   Arrive at the City Hall, New York.
Received by the Mayor.
Presentations.

3.45 p.m.   Leave the City Hall.

4.10 p.m.   Arrive at the Lincoln Centre.
Tour.

5.25 p.m.   Leave the Lincoln Centre.

TUESDAY 23 NOVEMBER

Private engagements.

WEDNESDAY 24 NOVEMBER

2.45 p.m.   Departure: Princess Margaret and Lord Snowdon arrive at J. F. Kennedy International Airport.

3.05 p.m.   Take off on BOAC's Flight No. BA 490 for Bermuda.

6.15 p.m.   Arrive at Bermuda.
Received by the Governor.
Presentations.

6.40 p.m.   Leave the Airport.
Short drive.

7 p.m.   Arrive at National Stadium.
Presentation of Colours to The Bermuda Regiment.

7.45 p.m.   Leave the National Stadium.

7.55 p.m.   Arrive at Government House.
Plant trees.
Cocktails.

8.50 p.m.   Dinner (18 people).

10.15 p.m.   Reception (120 people).

11.30 p.m.   Leave Government House.

11.59 p.m.   Leave Bermuda in BOAC's Flight No BA 696.

THURSDAY 25 NOVEMBER

10.30 a.m.   Arrive at London (Heathrow) Airport.

Bibliography

Princess Alice, Countess of Athlone,
Theo Aronson (Cassell, 1981)

*Royal Ambassadors: British Royalties in
South Africa 1860–1947*, Theo
Aronson (David Philip, Cape
Town, 1975)

The Story of Peter Townsend, Norman
Barrymaine (Peter Davies, 1958)

King George VI: His Life and Reign,
John W. Wheeler-Bennett
(Macmillan, 1958)

Margaret: The Tragic Princess, James
Brough (W. H. Allen, 1978)

*Self Portrait with Friends: The Selected
Diaries of Cecil Beaton 1926–1974*,
ed. Richard Buckle (Weidenfeld,
1979)

Princess Margaret, Helen Cathcart
(W. H. Allen, 1974)

The Little Princesses, Marion Crawford
(Odhams Press, 1950)

H.R.H. The Princess Margaret, Nigel
Dempster (Quartet, 1981)

My Queen and I, Willie Hamilton
(Quartet, 1975)

Queen Mary, James Pope-Hennessy
(Allen & Unwin, 1959)

*Chips: The Diaries of Sir Henry
Channon*, ed. Robert Rhodes James
(Weidenfeld, 1967)

The English Country House, A. F.
Kersting (Thames & Hudson,
1974)

The Queen Mother, Elizabeth Longford
(Weidenfeld, 1981)

The Noël Coward Diaries, Graham Payn
and Sheridan Morley (Weidenfeld,
1982)

Snowdon, David Sinclair (Proteus,
1982)

Time and Chance, Peter Townsend
(Collins, 1978)

Two Centuries of Royal Weddings,
Christopher Warwick (Arthur
Barker, 1980)

A King's Story, H.R.H. The Duke of
Windsor (Collins, 1951)

The Moment, essay entitled 'Royalty',
Virginia Woolf (Hogarth Press,
1947)

INDEX

SUSAN CROSLAND

TONY CROSLAND

'An intimate, witty, revealing but never cloying account of a disputatious public figure with an intensely-lived private life . . . painted so vividly that one feels like a fly, and a fascinated fly, on the wall.' *Sunday Times*

'A love story . . . it also tells you more about the man and his period than anything that has previously been written. Beside it, almost all contemporary political biography seems stilted and over-restrained.' *Financial Times*

'Essential reading . . . a fascinating story of a fascinating man' *The Listener*

'I do not remember reading another book that gives quite such a vivid impression of what it feels like to operate near the top levels of political leadership in a democracy.' *New York Times Book Review*

'An astonishing achievement, possibly the finest memoir of a British politician ever written.' *The Economist*

A Royal Mail service in association with the Book Marketing Council & The Booksellers Association

Post-A-Book is a Post Office trademark.

BERNARD LEVIN

CONDUCTED TOUR

A journey through twelve music festivals in Europe and Australia, from Adelaide to Wexford via Florence, Bath, Aldeburgh, Hohenems, Glyndebourne, Aix, Salzburg, Bayreuth, Edinburgh and Barcelona.

'The author declares that he has written not a music book, but a travel book. He is wrong. He has written a Levin book . . . compulsively readable.'

Punch

'Here is exhilarating writing about music . . . full of traveller's tales, it has all the beguiling charm that draws the eye to anything he writes.'

Sunday Telegraph

'Highly entertaining reading . . . delightful . . . the combination of substance of argument with lightness of touch is irresistible.'

Daily Telegraph

'Bernard Levin remains a master journalist.'

The Guardian

CORONET BOOKS

ALSO AVAILABLE FROM CORONET